LIFT

To fellow
entrepreneur
Samantha —
Martha John

LIFT

**How to Start, Run and Grow
Your Own Successful Business**

John & Martha King

Cover design by Ivica Jandrijevic
Interior layout and design by www.writingnights.org
Book preparation by Chad Robertson

ISBN: 978-0-9911957-9-4
LIBRARY OF CONGRESS CATALOGING-IN-PUBLICATION DATA:
NAMES: King, Martha & King, John, authors
TITLE: Lift – How to Start, Run and Grow Your Own
Successful Business / John & Martha King
DESCRIPTION: Independently Published, 2022
IDENTIFIERS: ISBN 9780991195794 (Perfect bound) |
SUBJECTS: | Non-Fiction | Entrepreneurship| Entrepreneurial Success | Aviation |
CLASSIFICATION: Pending
LC record pending

Independently Published
Printed in the United States of America.
Printed on acid-free paper.

24   23   22   21   20   19   18   17   8   7   6   5   4   3   2   1

DEDICATION

To David Jackson and Barry Knuttila,
who each in their own way
set us and King Schools up for success.

Give someone a fish and you feed them for a day.
Teach someone to fish and you feed them and their family for a lifetime.
—Entrepreneurial proverb

CONTENTS

CHAPTER 4 — TESTING YOUR CONCEPT FOR SUCCESS................... 53

CHAPTER 7 — USING SIMPLE, CREATIVE BUSINESS CONTROLS 113

CHAPTER 8 — MULTIPLYING YOUR EFFORTS THROUGH SMART HIRING...............131

INTRODUCTION

OUR PERSONAL STORY OF ENTREPRENEURSHIP

You have a wonderful opportunity. You live in a time and place where you can use entrepreneurship to improve your life and the lives you touch. This book is about helping you acquire the vision, motivation, and knowledge to take advantage of that opportunity. You will find included such necessary fundamentals as salesmanship and response marketing. These will help you gain the money that will serve as a lubricant to slide through life.

We are a couple who used entrepreneurship to allow us to work together in a business of providing knowledge courses to pilots. As technology progressed, we responded to feedback from our customers and put our interactive video courses on the internet, and as a result we have been able to teach half the pilots in the United States learning to fly.

As teachers of pilots, we have been fortunate to know many successful entrepreneurs who have been drawn to aviation. A few of these are billionaires, and we have come to deeply appreciate that entrepreneurs are problem-solvers who make life better for nearly everyone they touch. We believe entrepreneurship will be good for you and you will make it good for society. One of the strongest benefits you will receive is that entrepreneurship develops habits and aptitudes that will help you thrive and will facilitate your personal growth.

Entrepreneurship has been the centerpiece of our lives ever since we were married and became business partners more than five decades ago. One of the most important things we have learned in the process is that life as an entrepreneur can be deeply rewarding and fun.

At the outset of our marriage and partnership, we made the decision to be equal partners in everything we would do. We realized that it would be very unlikely that a company would hire us as equal partners, so we concluded that to be equal partners we had to be in business for ourselves.

Over the years, our concept of entrepreneurship has evolved. We began to understand that an entrepreneur becomes successful by seeking out and taking care of the needs of others. First is customers. Why would they volunteer to pay you money for goods or services unless those goods or services fulfilled their needs?

Next, why would employees devote substantial portions of their lives to your endeavor unless you fulfilled their needs? Even vendors need you to take care of their needs. Otherwise, why would they take the time to provide you goods and services?

Originally, we had a goal of making lots of money and being big-time operators. After we had a business failure and bankruptcy, we developed the philosophy that a major personal benefit of entrepreneurship is that it would not only allow us to work together but to also have meaningful and rewarding work providing a valuable service to pilots—customers we admired and cared about. We also felt that with our new goals, each of us would be a more valuable contributor and would be deeply fulfilled.

As our business developed, our business model evolved from providing aviation courses in classrooms to providing our aviation courses on video. Due to our commitment to be equal partners in everything we would do, we would both be teachers on our videos. Over time, teaching on video created the visibility that gave us both the opportunity and, we felt, the obligation to make a significant contribution to the aviation community. We learned to use evolving internet technology to make aviation learning more accessible and to help improve the risk-management practices of pilots. In our view, flying attracts very special people. When someone is learning to fly, it means a great deal to them. Entrepreneurship has given us the opportunity and privilege to play a role in the lives of so many very special people for whom flying means so much.

We feel very fortunate to have shared so much with each other through the years. One of the things we have especially enjoyed is flying together in jet airplanes that require two pilots. It feels to us as if we are dancing a graceful ballet together.

Flying well as a crew requires that we demonstrate mutual respect:

- We address the pilot in command as "captain," no matter which one of us it is.
- The captain must solicit input from the monitoring pilot.
- The monitoring pilot has to be respectful about their input, and give information but not opinions.

The crew resource management required in flying a two-pilot airplane has been helpful to us in all aspects of our partnership, especially our business.

Ironically, after we moved away from the goals of making lots of money and being "big-time operators," technology and entrepreneurship enabled us to scale our business to the point where we were teaching half the pilots learning to fly in the United States. Plus, we became monetarily successful enough to fly our own corporate jet without financial strain.

We've been broke (bankrupt) and not broke—we like not broke a lot better. We have learned that being in a business failure and running out of cash makes everything more difficult. On the other hand, success gives you money, which as we said earlier is a lubricant that lets you slide through life. Just as everything is more difficult when you are failing, everything is easier when you're succeeding. Most importantly, we have learned that entrepreneurial success is deeply satisfying and rewarding in a way that most jobs just can't ever be.

Success opens many doors for you, even in unrelated areas. For instance, our work as teachers in the aviation community has opened the world at the highest levels to us. We have played a role in the lives of incredible people from billionaires (including Ray Dolby) and Hollywood personalities (including Clint Eastwood) to famous pilots (including Chuck Yeager), political figures (including Betty Ford), journalists (including Walter Cronkite), and many more. You will learn about our associations with them in sidebars throughout this book.

You will likely enjoy your entrepreneurial journey the most if you combine it with something you have a passion for. Pursuing a passion will make everything you do more fun. You will work harder and longer and be more willing to persist through difficulties. That persistence greatly improves the odds of your achieving profitability. (Of course, that passion needs to be something that can be profitable.)

Time is your most precious commodity. You will want to look back at the end of your life and be able to say that you spent this most precious commodity on something about which you care deeply.

In our case, we have a passion for aircraft and people who fly. That passion fits in with our interest in business. To us, flying airplanes and conducting business are similar in that both leverage intelligent planning and design, coupled with knowledgeable people at the helm, to move quickly to goals.

In the same way that the shape of an airplane wing, along with the design of the engines and the rest of the plane, operated by a skilled and knowledgeable pilot, allows the pilot, passengers, and cargo to move forward and then, almost magically, be lifted into the air for a beautiful, efficient, fun journey, the correct structure of a business, led by a knowledgeable entrepreneur, can improve lives and deliver products and services to people at a price they're happy to pay.

No matter how brief the flight, there are always little things (sometimes big things) that will require corrections in order to have a successful journey. If there's a wind that's pushing you slightly off course, you make slight adjustments to land at the airport you had in mind. Those little corrections are no big deal, but without them you could end up landing where you did not intend.

John and Martha flew their C340 on a circuit of cities when conducting weekend ground schools.

In flying and in business, you'll always need to make corrections along the way. But in flying, when you are a good pilot in a well-built plane—just like when you're a good entrepreneur running a well-designed company—you can make progress others only dream of.

To sum up our feeling about entrepreneurship: It has allowed us to serve a community of people who we care deeply about, and to do very well financially in the process. We heartily recommend entrepreneurship. It caused us to grow personally, and it provides meaningful, rewarding work serving people we have chosen to serve because we care about them. We hope entrepreneurship will do the same for you.

In this book, we will do our best to give you tools that we hope will enable you to provide valuable and profitable products and services to the people you care about.

John & Martha King

CHAPTER

1

THE GIFT AND IMPORTANCE OF ENTREPRENEURSHIP

Your choice to be an entrepreneur will forever change your habits and perception of who you are and how you feel about yourself—all of which together is known as your paradigm. As a result, you will improve the lives of those you touch—your fellow workers, your customers, and your vendors. You will change their lives because you, as an entrepreneur, will have thought carefully about what their needs are and how you can take care of them. That is the reason you will be able to engage successfully with them.

Successful entrepreneurs make a profit by thinking carefully about how to help others and how to solve problems. Making a profit is a good thing. Making money from doing good things for others doesn't make the effort any less legitimate or ethical. It makes the work viable and makes it possible to provide employment to one's own employees and to pay vendors, who then pay their own employees.

The wealth gained from profit becomes a tool to expand the business to do more good things for others.

The purpose of this book is to help you become a successful entrepreneur. If you want to be a successful entrepreneur, we encourage you to embrace and incorporate the principles we share in this book. In later chapters, we will share various fundamentals of entrepreneurship that we believe will help you be a much more successful entrepreneur. Success in business comes from doing something that is very important to you and working hard at it. In the process, you will have taken care of the needs of others.

Our conviction and experience is that entrepreneurs are hard workers who approach the world as problem-solvers and who, in the process, create abundance and put countless people to productive work.

This book will supply you with a series of fundamental principles coupled with a servant-leadership approach to business, along with a sequence of contingency plans for dealing with the variables in your business. Sure, you can get rich, and it may even be quick. But what you will learn here will not be a get-rich-quick scheme, but instead the entrepreneurial principles, skills, and methods that have taken us nearly five decades to learn in our own business.

You will come to realize that our definition of a successful business is "the identification of a customer's need or want that you can fulfill profitably." When you can profitably and ethically help others gain something, save money, avoid trouble, or solve a problem at a price they are willing to pay, you have the foundation for a viable and rewarding business.

Providing true value to customers is, we believe, the first and most important principle of entrepreneurship. Success will result, we believe, from building on a foundation of seeking out and taking care of needs, coupled with your personal passion for your business.

It is every entrepreneur's pursuit of an interest or passion that allows them to understand the needs of a potential community or industry well enough to identify and supply a product or service that provides such value that the customer is willing to pay for it.

Additionally, that same entrepreneur has developed an understanding of the needs of potential qualified employees well enough to attract them to work in collaboration with the entrepreneur, and the entrepreneur has developed an understanding of the needs of vendors well enough to elicit their cooperation.

Everyone benefits from the efforts of the entrepreneur. Customers receive the value from the product or service. Employees of the business are provided with meaningful and rewarding work, as well as income. Vendors serving the business are also earning income and their employees are earning a living. Taxes (not to mention charitable donations) provided by entrepreneurs and vendors, plus those paid by the entrepreneur's and vendors' employees, are all contributing to the betterment of the local and national community and society at large.

A helpful way to understand how entrepreneurs become wealthy is to understand that each sale to a customer is a request for that customer's voluntary vote of support in which the customer has voted "yes." In fact, the way many very wealthy people have become wealthy is that they asked society to vote for them by buying their product or service. Because of the value the business provided, selected members of the public (their customers) voted personally and directly with their hard-earned dollars to make these entrepreneurs wealthy.

Here's what we mean.

One of the greatest contributions to society in modern times is the smartphone. Billions of people the world over have one in their pocket right now. Through the invention of the internet, the smartphone instantly makes available virtually all the knowledge in the world to these billions, plus many other services such as GPS location services, still and video cameras, music players, newspapers, and many, many others.

One of the most profitable companies in America today is Apple. The company's founder, Steve Jobs, was one of the wealthiest people in America and highest-paid CEO. Tim Cook, Apple's current CEO, is following in Steve's footsteps.

Apple's current success was not necessarily a slam-dunk. When Apple started out, it was one of several companies developing computers and the operating systems to run them. Over the years, they adjusted their business model in ways many people don't even remember. They licensed the Mac Operating System (OS), and other hardware companies made Mac-compatible computers for a while (today, only Apple makes Apple computers). Apple tried its hand at the personal digital assistant (PDA) business, developing the Apple Newton to compete with Palm Pilots. Around the time Palm entered the newly emerging smartphone market, Apple had discontinued Newtons and released the first iPhone. That smartphone had a mere fraction of the features and functions of modern iPhones, and countless cell phone competitors were all fighting for their piece of the pie.

Today, Apple makes the most popular, best-selling collection of smartphones on the planet, and their computer, tablet, and software sales are also robust. Its ascension to market leader wasn't without some missteps. But ultimately they have created hardware and software that people want so much, they are happy to stand in line overnight to be the first to own new Apple products.

Apple is responsible for happy customers who voted with their own money to make Apple the market leader. Apple is also responsible for the successful careers of their employees. The company is the reason countless software developers earn a living, including some who work at King Schools. Apple pays vendors for parts and manufacturing. Apple pays for real estate, office construction, and property taxes. And numerous Apple employees have founded their own tech companies, in turn creating well-paying jobs for others.

To continue to grow as a company and develop new products that people wanted, Apple had to make profits in the first place. They made computers and software that people wanted - and the people were willing to pay the requested price. Apple did not develop the Mac, Newton, iPad, Apple Watch, or iPhone with money confiscated from taxpayers and by receiving government grants. It is the most successful company in the United States because it sells things at a price that is both profitable for the company and that a large-enough portion of the population is willing to pay.

HYPOTHETICAL "FAIRNESS" WEALTH CONFISCATION

If you believe that some arbitrary limit of profit or personal income should exist, consider this: New products are developed using profits from previous sales. If profit confiscation had been in effect in Apple's early days, it's possible the iPhone would never have been invented.

"No big deal," you say. "The world would still be moving on without the iPhone." True. But isn't the world better off *with* an iPhone? It may appear to be expensive, but consider all the things it provides to iPhone users: Full access to the world of information on the internet. Voice commands for countless tasks. Mobile connectivity to family and employers. Time-saving navigation aids. Health aids and even life-saving services. Digital photography and video capture for work, play, communications, record-keeping, and more. The iPhone has been instrumental in bringing the world together on a very personal level.

And don't even think for a minute that if Apple hadn't invented it, someone else would have. Not if that "excess wealth/profit confiscation" plan had been in play. If all companies making sufficient profits to fund R&D and the manufacturing of new inventions were taxed to make things "fair," it's likely no one would have the resources to make an iPhone-like competitor.

CHARITABLE CONTRIBUTIONS

The assumption that all wealthy people are greedy rarely takes into consideration that contributions to charities of every type come from people with sufficient income to support charities they believe in. People fail to take into consideration that confiscation of "excess" profits or salaries would likely halt R&D and innovation and would certainly crush voluntary charitable contributions from those same profitable companies and well-paid executives and staff.

Consider for a moment the current world. Isn't it better off with modern smartphones? Aren't charities better off with big corporate and personal donations?

As it turns out, having the government step in to "make things fair" would likely cause far more society-wide damage and economic stagnation, if not outright poverty, than most people could even imagine.

TRUSTWORTHINESS AS AN ENTREPRENEURIAL PILLAR

When entrepreneurs are successful, they have achieved success, in almost every case, by displaying the element of trustworthiness. People are trustworthy when they respect others, have the interests of others at heart, are predictable, and play by fair rules. The reason one can almost be certain that successful entrepreneurs are trustworthy is that if they weren't, they wouldn't obtain the collaboration they need from customers, fellow workers, and vendors.

As a result, when you endeavor to be truthful and ethical in your approach to business—in short, trustworthy—you are far more likely to succeed. Ethical companies build a loyal customer base, and in difficult times, loyal customers, employees, and vendors can keep a business moving ahead.

SUMMARY

The core of any worthwhile entrepreneurial venture should be a positive, ethical approach to ensure everyone is better off for having engaged in the process. This includes customers, employees, vendors, and the entrepreneurs themselves. When entrepreneurship is based on a trustworthy approach to all aspects of a business, everyone will be better off for having been a part of this company and its transactions. Successful entrepreneurs are helpful, thoughtful, generous problem-solvers, and the world is a better place because of their efforts.

Now let's explore steps you can take to use your passions and knowledge to make everyone you come in touch with better off.

CHAPTER

2

PURSUE YOUR PASSIONS, NOT A PAYCHECK

Your parents and your teachers lied to you. They told you the best way to get ahead was to get a good job with a reliable company. Put in your time. Save your money. And someday, if you live long enough, you could retire. That's what they believed. But take a little deeper look at the way they say things work and you'll see there's nothing in that picture they painted about having fun.

Talk about demotivating! There's nothing in that plan that encourages you. And the whole time you live the life of an employee, you're at the mercy of countless events that are outside your control. At a minimum, the company is managed to benefit the company or the manager. The focus is not on you.

We're not saying your parents or teachers had some sort of ill intent. It's just what they knew. In most cases, they were not only lying to you, they were lying to themselves. They heard and believed that getting a "good job" was the smart path to success. The truth is, there's a much better path than the employee route, one that helps people enjoy the journey to even greater success. It's a path that gives you more power and more freedom. The challenges are greater than just holding down a 9-to-5 job, but the rewards are huge, and well beyond simple financial gains. And the big secret is that when you do it right, it's incredibly fun!

THE HARD-AND-FAST RULES FOR SUCCESS ACCORDING TO SUCCESSFUL ENTREPRENEURS

We took a course at Indiana University called "Enterprise and Entrepreneurship" from a professor named Bill Haeberle, and the class sessions were at Bill's house. Bill was a champion of entrepreneurship and every week we would meet in this informal environment with our classmates and Bill, along with a different entrepreneur he had invited to talk with our class. This was a fantastic learning opportunity and it informed a lot of our views on entrepreneurship.

The class was much less formal and structured than a normal classroom setting. The visiting entrepreneur would start out having a nice dinner with Bill beforehand, and due to informal conversation and an enjoyable meal, along with a few drinks with dinner, these entrepreneurs would be ready to go in casual-conversation mode rather than business-presentation mode. Then we would arrive with our classmates after dinner and find the guests were generally very relaxed. We'd all sit and listen to each entrepreneur as Bill prompted them with interview-style questions. One of the key questions Bill was sure to ask at these meetings was what each entrepreneur believed were "the hard-and-fast rules for success."

Over the course of the semester, dozens of fantastic, successful entrepreneurs shared their thoughts, and through this learning experience, we discovered that each entrepreneur had a different set of "hard and fast" rules for success. As a class, we would study the answers for commonalities and look for useful insights, but it was eye-opening for our entire class to realize that each entrepreneur had their own unique style and their own set of motivating beliefs, without a lot of overlap.

One evening, our featured guest was the president of Martin Marietta, a leading defense contractor during World War II. After introducing him to our class, Bill asked an open-ended interview-style question: "Talk to us about the challenges that Martin Marietta faced at the end of World War II. You had all these military contracts and suddenly all that business was gone."

The president briefly discussed how various teams at Martin Marietta were moved around and how management focused on adjusting workflows and sales to keep as many employees as possible, all while generating new streams of income. Then he shifted gears from logistics. He spoke directly to the class with a piece of advice that has stayed with us to this day. He said, "Don't ever depend on anyone else for your security."

He continued, "I have ten thousand people working for me, and week after week after week I have not been sure that we would still be in business by the next week. And all these people thought they had security because they were working for a big company. They had no clue how unsecure they really were."

It wasn't just surprising that he shared this amazing admission, it was also eye-opening that he was eager to have all of us become entrepreneurs and not depend on a big company. The president of Martin Marietta, who employed ten thousand people, was a champion for entrepreneurship.

ENTREPRENEURS AREN'T NORMAL

You're not normal. Normal people don't have the courage it takes to follow their passion, because they're afraid they will fail.

You want to be an entrepreneur, and your fears of failure aren't enough to hold you back. You have the courage to pursue your passion. You're pursuing entrepreneurship even though failure could be the result.

Our focus on learning has been a big part of our makeup throughout our lives. Before we ever met, we were both dedicated students and valedictorians at our respective high schools. When we met during our college years, we continued to study and learn all we could about the subjects we planned to use in our adult lives as a newly married couple and beyond. These days, we still love learning.

But no matter how hard you study and how much you plan and prepare for future potential problems—even if you're a valedictorian— you can't learn everything you'll need for your entrepreneurial journey in a classroom or from a book. That doesn't mean you shouldn't pay attention in school and try to learn all you can about business. It just means that as an entrepreneur, you should plan to be a lifelong student. You should also have contingency plans to make necessary changes and improvements along the way.

The good news is that every generation builds on what came before them and adds their own new experiences and knowledge to current educational curricula. Classes on every area of study today are far more informed—and usually much more advanced and accurate—than those same topics taught to previous generations. A mechanical engineer graduating today from the same university where her father got his mechanical engineering degree thirty years ago has learned things her father could only have dreamed of as a student.

Our goal with this book is not only to share the many foundational principles of entrepreneurship we learned in school and put into practice in our business, but also to add our personal experience and realizations. We offer updated approaches to business so that today's entrepreneurs can benefit from our experience. Interestingly, some of our discoveries aren't being taught in school even today. The best way to look at our teaching in this book is to understand that these are *our* "hard and fast" rules for success in entrepreneurship. And you can't trust us either. Rather than relying on us, you should think through your own "hard and fast rules for success."

HAVING FUN IS THE KEY TO GETTING AHEAD

People get ahead more in business and in life when the journey is fun. Your business ventures should be fun.

It's important that you understand we're not pushing some sort of positive-thinking formula for getting rich. We're just telling you the truth. Entrepreneurship is not easy. Building a successful business requires a lot of work and energy. Entrepreneurs need to work hard and they need to be committed students who never stop learning. You need to be having fun, because if you're not having fun, you'll lose motivation and won't get important work done.

When you are having fun, you'll work harder. You'll be more interested in your business and your industry, and you'll continue to learn more. You'll continue to advance. So you need to plan your entrepreneurial journey around something that is a passion of yours. Something that fills you with energy and excitement. Something that encourages you to keep pushing forward even when others might quit. Chase your passions, not money.

A word of warning, though: Pursuing your passion will turn up the intensity knob of life. You'll be working a lot harder, but you'll get more out of everything you do. And that knowledge and effort will give you power. It will give you personal freedom and control. It will mean financial rewards and social rewards.

A truth we've learned over the years is:

"Life and entrepreneurship reward knowledgeable people who put effort into what they do."

You might read that statement and consider it just a platitude or our opinion, but once you're on your entrepreneurial journey and you look back, you'll realize you've been rewarded for your passion and the work you've put in. You'll experience the payoff of your committed passion.

"SCRABBLE LETTERS" ARE LIFE AND BUSINESS SKILLS

When people hear the word "Scrabble," most instantly think of the board game with letter tiles that has been around for generations.

The way the Scrabble board game works is that the more valuable letter tiles you have, the more valuable words you can spell in the board game. And the more valuable words you can spell, the higher you will score. The secret to winning the game is to spell valuable words.

Now in the board game Scrabble, you only get seven letter tiles. And you don't get to choose the letters, you draw the tiles blindly from the pile. But the good news is that in the game of life it's much different. You can have as many Scrabble tiles as you want, and you get to choose what the letters will be, based on your interests and passions.

Our Scrabble analogy is that areas in life and business that you know more about than others are like valuable Scrabble letters. The more areas of knowledge you know, the more successful business ideas you can put together, and the better you will do. Accordingly, one goal of an entrepreneur should be to develop areas of knowledge you know more about than other people so you can put them together to make winning business ideas.

At this point, even if you haven't started a business yet, you are sure to have some valuable "Scrabble letters." Maybe you're really good at public speaking. Maybe you can create websites that look fantastic. Maybe you're a great salesperson. These are all what we call valuable Scrabble letters and each of these skills can join with other skills to create successful businesses.

On the other hand, maybe you have a Scrabble tile like a passion about smartphone technology or modern music. These passions might not seem like they can help you in business right away, but at some time in the future, those Scrabble letters might combine with something else to be helpful after all. The goal is two-fold: Always be collecting valuable Scrabble letters and always be looking for ways to combine your letters so you can create valuable words.

In our case, we made a successful business out of teaching aviation ground schools. Here is our story in Scrabble letters:

AVIATION, our first passion, and our first valuable Scrabble letter, let us develop knowledge we could teach.

TEACHING let us conduct small aviation ground-school classes based on our knowledge.

DIRECT MAIL allowed us to advertise, which enabled large ground-school classes.

VIDEO created a product we could send out.

COMPUTERIZED LEARNING made it much easier for students to learn.

INTERNET COURSE DELIVERY made the learning mobile and even easier for students.

INTERNET MARKETING made it easier for customers to buy our services.

It doesn't take much insight for people to understand how these letters—our skill sets—interplay to create the structure of our business. Our Scrabble letters spelled out b-u-s-i-n-e-s-s s-u-c-c-e-s-s for us.

What's interesting, though, is that in our case, flying is a core passion that motivates us and gives us energy, and teaching is a secondary passion that allows us to share our aviation passion with others and earn a generous living doing it.

Two of our Scrabble letters, direct mail and video, are areas of interest that we turned into areas of deeper learning, and eventually we learned enough to be able to call them areas of expertise. While they may not be the emotional-level, driving passion that aviation is for us, they became Scrabble letters that helped grow our business.

If you understand that our passion for flying is a true driving force that energizes us and makes us excited to wake up every morning—but on its own, loving to fly doesn't pay the bills—you start to understand that a Scrabble letter of your passion will power your forward momentum in collecting other Scrabble letters. Then, a good combination of additional skills can combine with your deep passion to become a profitable business.

PLAY WITH TNT

You've heard that if you play with fire you might get burned—we recommend PLAY with TNT instead.

As trainers, we use learning tools and memory aids like acronyms and mnemonics all the time. That's where PLAY and TNT came from, and they will help you on your Scrabble letters journey.

"PLAY" is a word we use to remind entrepreneurs of habits that will help you acquire more and more valuable Scrabble letters over time. "TNT" is a term we use to help you remember how to organize your Scrabble letters to make a dynamite business.

PLAY stands for the habits of:

- **Passion:** Successful entrepreneurs need a passion.
- **Lots of interests** help you develop more passions.

- **Always learning**: A deeper knowledge of topics turns interests into Scrabble letters.
- **Yet again**: Repeat these behaviors until they become habits.

Following these habits will help you get valuable Scrabble Letters.

Most important, you need a strong passion. You need to build your business around something that energizes you while you're working and keeps you moving forward when it seems like things are going wrong.

If you have two or three or five strong passions, great! Don't worry yet about which one should be the one that drives your business. The value of specific Scrabble letters is based on the words you can create by combining them with other Scrabble letters. Your passionate pursuit won't be standing on its own—it will be part of the bigger picture. We'll dive into the ways you can decide which passion to pursue later on in this book.

If you don't think you have one single passion that could light your entrepreneurial fire, you probably actually do, but you've just told yourself, "Nobody would pay me to do that," or "There's no way to turn that into a business."

Here's a little booster exercise to open your mind a bit. Read this sentence and fill in the blank:

"If I could wake up every day and get paid to _____, my life would be fantastic!"

If nothing comes to mind, keep reading this book but put a book-mark here and come back to it and read the sentence again later. Read it when you first wake up and see what comes to mind. Read it in front of your friends or your spouse or relationship partner and ask them to fill in the blank with what they think your passion is. Just keep coming back to this exercise from time to time and you'll generate answers that will highlight your passions.

HEY, ENTREPRENEURS! GRAB THESE CRITICAL SCRABBLE TILES!

Collecting more valuable Scrabble tiles is always a good goal and a fun part of life. Regardless of your current collection of Scrabble letters, every entrepreneur needs the following three letters (skill sets) in their collection (we will elaborate on these in later chapters):

- Salesmanship
- Response marketing
- Ability to create outstanding customer experiences

SCRABBLE LETTERS MEAN BUSINESS WITH TNT

Remember that PLAY refers to your interests and behaviors that will help you acquire more valuable Scrabble letters over time. TNT stands for things that will help you sell your Scrabble letters:

- **Trust:** Be a trustworthy person.
- **Needs:** Seek out the needs of others.
- **Triumph:** With solutions to those needs.

Trust: Being a trustworthy person is necessary to get people to be willing to depend on you. People trust someone who they think respects them and has their interests at heart, is predictable and plays by fair rules.

Needs: The way entrepreneurs get ahead is by seeking out and taking care of the needs of others. A good way to find those needs is to remember what we are all thinking all the time, and that is "What's in it for me?" We call that "WIIFM."

Triumph: The final **T** refers to a triumph with solutions to the needs of others.

Put your Scrabble letters together in ways that meet the needs you have discovered and you'll have solutions that provide a profit.

In the end, your true entrepreneurial success will come from the words you create with your Scrabble letters to apply "TNT." Greater success happens when you have more Scrabble letters that can be combined to make even more words. And, of course, with our Scrabble analogy, more "words" means more avenues for entrepreneurial success.

Collecting Scrabble letters needs to become a skill set in and of itself. Pursuing knowledge pays off in ways you could never anticipate. Until you actually acquire a new Scrabble letter, you don't know how it might be combined with other Scrabble letters in your collection and how valuable it will become.

OUR FLIGHT OVER THE NORTH ATLANTIC AND HOW THE RESULTING SCRABBLE LETTERS SPELLED "SUCCESS"

In 2004, we flew our plane on an incredible fourteen-day around-the-world journey over Canada to Greenland, over the North Atlantic to Iceland, then to Norway, Moscow, through Russia and Alaska, and back home to California. The reason for the trip was multifold: We love flying. We love learning. And we love experiencing new places and other cultures.

Khabarovsk is in the Russian Far East, east of Manchuria on the Amur River.

The learning component was especially interesting to us because of the required pilot certifications and enhanced skill set needed for navigation in places where we had never flown before. Not only did we need to understand alternate emergency procedures over the North Atlantic and metric (instead of feet) measurements used by air traffic control in Russia, we also had to work with a different high-altitude safety standard referred to as "reduced vertical separation minimums" (RVSM).

If you're not a pilot, here's an explanation. Based on the direction you're flying, air traffic control will assign you an altitude and you must maintain that altitude accurately in order to avoid coming dangerously close vertically to other aircraft. If you're flying in an easterly direction, you will be assigned an altitude with an odd number of thousands of feet (such as 31,000 or 35,000 feet). If you're flying in a westerly direction, you can expect an altitude assignment of an even number of thousands of feet (such as 32,000 feet or 34,000 feet). For safety, you must maintain that altitude as precisely as possible.

At the time we took our Russia trip, the vertical separation minimum between planes in the United States was 2,000 feet for a pilot flying at an altitude of 29,000 feet and higher. Below 29,000 feet, you could expect a vertical separation minimum of 1,000 feet. The lower number is because altimeters operate based on air pressure, and the reduced air pressure at higher altitudes means that at high altitudes, altimeters are intrinsically less accurate. Some planes just didn't have accurate-enough altimeter readings to safely maintain their assigned altitude if the separation was only 1,000 feet. Those high-altitude increased vertical minimums of 2,000 feet were a safety measure.

In 2004, over the North Atlantic, RVSMs were in effect. The reduction to 1,000 feet separation above 29,000 feet of altitude required additional airplane equipment, certification of the aircraft's altimetry system, special maintenance procedures, and additional pilot training. The training we received from an online Australian course resulted in a certification that allowed us to fly in that North Atlantic RVSM airspace.

The learning was rewarding and the trip created wonderful memories. But it was an investment of time, education, and travel expenses. Altogether we spent around $50,000 to enjoy our trip to the other side of the globe. We traveled in style in our own jet and with a guide at each location we visited.

When we got back to San Diego, we spent a little time creating a course about RVSM for other pilots who might be flying over the North Atlantic. We didn't expect this to be a big market, but we thought there would be some level of interest. Six months after our trip, the United States adopted the same RVSM procedures for U.S. domestic airspace. We had a little warning that this new standard was on the way, so we polished our brand-new course a little and put it out there for pilots across the United States who would need this new certification.

At the time, a few other educators in the United States had classes with similar content, but they were live, all-day classes. That required pilots to take time away from work to attend and travel to the class location. It was also an expensive in-person class in the $800–$900 range. Interestingly, that all-day class was only necessary because of all the additional regulations and procedures necessary to fly over the North Atlantic. On the other hand, just the RVSM procedures for the new U.S. standards were easy enough to teach in about an hour, and that's all the majority of pilots wanted. We charged less for our course, much less than the others charged for a full-day in-person class, and we made it available online. Our class came with a certificate and a log-book endorsement sticker when students finished the course.

Keep in mind that learning everything we needed to get our fly-around-the-world Scrabble letters required an investment of just under $50K. When we made that investment, we had no idea it might become a profitable Scrabble letter, but in 2005, the first full year we sold our RVSM course in the United States, we took in a gross margin of $327,974 with very few expenses. It's a great example of how learning new areas of knowledge can end up being profitable.

3

HOW TO DESIGN YOUR WINNING BUSINESS

You will most likely find that identifying a customer need or want you can fulfill profitably is not a slam-dunk process. It takes a thorough understanding of your potential customer and their needs and wants. That is why getting Scrabble letters is so helpful. Every area in which you know more than other people gives you a better understanding of potential customers' needs and wants.

FIGURING OUT NEEDS OR WANTS IS NOT EASY

But understanding needs and wants can be tricky. Even when you are looking at successful businesses, you may not find it easy to figure out exactly what customer need or want they are fulfilling.

For instance, we have never found it easy to figure out what need or want the very successful Starbucks chain is satisfying. Most people acknowledge that Starbucks is selling far more than coffee and related food. Some say they are selling a "third place" where people can go to work and think. Others say they are selling a connection to the intellectuality of ancient coffee houses. The entrepreneurs who started Starbucks had a lot of thinking to do about what they were really selling.

When you are designing your winning business, you will want to do similar serious thinking about what need or want you will be fulfilling.

While we are talking about how to design a winning business, you may find it beneficial to consider how we failed at designing the concept for our first business. We decided, for our first concept, to provide customers with mobile refueling services and later mobile lubrication services by establishing franchises around the country. Our thought was that we were fulfilling the customers' need to have these services on a much more efficient, convenient, and money-saving basis—and our customers told us we were doing that.

We had also spent some time thinking about the risk of a fixed location. We were considering the life experience from the family business John grew up with, King's One Stop service station and restaurant. In its heyday, King's One Stop (started and run by John's parents) was successful because it was on Route 40, the national highway that once traversed the entire country. Thousands upon thousands of travelers going east or west across the middle of the country would see this nice service station and attached restaurant and stop in because it was convenient. That business and the associated real estate became virtually worthless when a new interstate highway drained the traffic from Route 40. The U.S. interstate project changed everything about how people traveled, and the number of travelers driving by King's One Stop dropped dramatically. Our idea of a portable service to customers was designed, in part, to eliminate the risks of a fixed location.

We had both been diligent students in business school and had learned from some of the most successful executives in the country. Additionally, John had extensive life experience in business from having participated in the family business. Life experience coupled with excellent education and planning gave us confidence that we had designed a winning business.

We were wrong, and we went broke.

We went wrong in several ways:

- We were not passionate about the business, and that limited our willingness to persist through difficulty.
- We hadn't designed sufficient protections into our relationships with our franchisees.
- We were selling products and services that customers could easily go elsewhere to replace.
- We were defective in our goal setting.

Our mobile refueling business, which we called TankLine, borrowed from the limited knowledge John had from growing up in the gas station business. Essentially, we created a gas station on wheels. We would go to warehouse locations where there were a few trucks, or maybe even dozens, and we would refuel the vehicles onsite, saving the business the mileage and the time to refuel their vehicles. That could really add up to big savings for some commercial clients.

Where John's background in the gas station business paid off is that we understood the pricing system of retail gasoline sales. We wanted the same pricing that rural distributers who sold to gas stations paid for their gasoline. Being the brash young kids we were, we wrote letters to the presidents of twenty-one oil companies. Texaco responded with the distributor pricing we were seeking, plus other support. It made the margins workable for us.

We recruited local college students as sales staff to call on fleet operators, but we wanted to increase our customer base beyond operators of commercial trucks—we wanted to refuel personal cars as well. In those days there weren't nearly as many convenient gas stations as there are today, and people had to be more deliberate about their refueling. When our college salespeople weren't calling on commercial clients, we had them calling on apartment complexes where there were a lot of cars parked in a small area. We had a little additional success with that, but we were still looking for more growth opportunities. One of our primary guiding principles in those days was "Growth Is Good."

During one of our refueling stops for a commercial customer, a manager asked us if we could do oil change and lubrication service for them also. He said they were happy enough with the refueling, but it wasn't really that much help to them. On the other hand, if we could provide the oil and lube service after hours, that would mean their trucks wouldn't have to be out of service during the workday for this kind of standard maintenance. That would be a really big help to them.

That was a lightbulb moment for us. We knew we could easily add that kind of service, and with a little examination we discovered it could be more profitable for us than just refilling gas tanks. It wasn't long before we were running a mobile oil change and lubrication service and enjoying new clients and increased profits.

We began to set goals for growth, initially deciding we wanted fifty franchisees nationwide. (Notice we did not consider *profitable* growth.)

Franchising was a matter of finding someone who would be willing to buy a specially designed service truck from us for the oil and lube business. We would give the business operator a contract for discounted product prices, training, our national customers, and our continuous help with marketing and sales.

Our franchising company was called American FleetCare Systems, Inc., and it was a good business for everyone involved. We were all profitable and American FleetCare was on its way to our fifty-franchisee goal. Then something happened that we never could have predicted.

In 1973, an oil embargo imposed by members of the Organization of Petroleum Exporting Countries (OPEC) led to fuel shortages and sky-high fuel prices. Under these circumstances, the weaknesses in our business structure became very noticeable. The franchisees had a problem because gas stations had long lines and sometimes only sold fuel to their customers on odd or even days. Many gas stations demanded that fleet customers buy their lubrication services from the station, or the station wouldn't sell them gas. This really hurt the sales of our franchisees. Consequently, the franchisees had a meeting and agreed to no longer pay American FleetCare the license fees they owed us.

Without the money they owed us, we couldn't pay for our own expenses or continue with our own business.

The problem was compounded by the fact that we had no leverage over our franchisees. Unlike many franchising companies, we had no way to enforce our contract. Many retail franchisers own the real estate where the business operates, and paying franchise fees is part of the lease. If the franchisee doesn't pay those fees, they can be evicted from the property. We had no such mechanism and no way to enforce the collection of our fees.

On top of that, the franchisees were selling products and services that their customers could easily obtain elsewhere. This limited the value we provided the franchisees and the profitability of our company.

The franchisees were in hard times and there was very little we could do to help them. The problems were bigger than our company, even bigger than our country, and we had no solutions for them.

It wasn't long before we realized that our oil and lube business and all our franchisees would soon be out of business and we would be broke. And that's exactly what happened.

WE LEARNED A LOT FROM THE FAILURE

We couldn't have predicted the OPEC oil embargo and there really wasn't much we could have done about it, but there were several lessons to be learned from the experience:

- We were selling products and services that were close to commodities and were easily replaceable—if we'd had irreplaceable products and services, we would have been less vulnerable.

- We had set goals for growth, but not profitability—had we been more profitable, we might have been able to survive through the difficult time.
- We didn't have the kind of passion for the truck lubrication business that we later had for our aviation business—if we'd had that kind of passion, we could have persisted longer. Our passion for our aviation business allowed us to develop a product that is irreplaceable.
- We had a business design without adequate protections for the company—better protections might have allowed us to last.

Even if we had done everything perfectly, it is not likely our business would have survived the OPEC oil embargo. But these lessons helped us design a profitable and robust business in the future.

OUR PASSION FOR FLYING IS AT THE HEART OF OUR ULTIMATE ENTREPRENEURIAL SUCCESS

From our current vantage point, we can easily see a number of reasons our previous business went broke, but the one that stands out the most is our lack of passion for truck lubrication. The day-to-day operation of the business simply wasn't fun for us. Our general passion for business and marketing wasn't enough to maintain success through hard times. And while it didn't happen right away, our next business's success as the leading pilot-training company in the country came about because of our passion for flying. We enjoy everything about flying and being around pilots and aircraft. Plus, the fact that we are the instructors on our videos means that we cannot easily be replicated or replaced.

DON'T JUST FOLLOW YOUR PASSION. COLLECT SCRABBLE LETTERS, THEN DESIGN A WINNING BUSINESS!

As folks who have been broke and then not broke because of our business ventures, it's frustrating to see authors and internet gurus telling people, "All you have to do to be successful is follow your passion. Pursue your passion and the world will make you rich and happy beyond your wildest dreams." In the real world, passion just isn't enough. We talk about the importance of passion, but that's only part of the puzzle.

As we discussed in Chapter Two, we call the knowledge gained from pursuing passions "Scrabble letters." We have found that you need to develop a number of passions, then find a combination of your Scrabble letters that can deliver products or services for which people are happy to give you their hard-earned money. Just because we loved flying didn't mean that flying alone would deliver income. And we didn't have a desire to be pilots for a commercial airline or even fly planes owned by private companies. Instead, we combined our passion for flying with our business passions and our passion for continued learning and teaching. By doing so, we designed a winning business.

Over the years, we have collected quite a few tools and strategies to help fellow entrepreneurs along their journey, and as you might imagine, we hope we have quite a few insights that can help you design your winning business.

As we said earlier, what you are looking for is a way you can profitably and ethically help others gain something, save money, avoid trouble, or solve a problem at a price they are willing to pay. Having a knowledge of others' situations helps in this search. That knowledge is a big part of the Scrabble letters that you can put together for solutions.

You can start by looking for change. Consider that you could always go into a line of business that already exists, but if you're just like everyone else in that field, you'll be fighting an uphill battle to gain market share. On the other hand, if you see a change coming in an industry or community where you have some Scrabble letters, you could potentially leverage that to create a new, unique offering that others haven't yet presented. Creating a niche where customers can't easily replace your product or service is a great place to start!

FedEx is a famous example of a slight twist to existing services that opened a whole new market. Plenty of companies (including the U.S. Postal Service) already shipped products and paperwork from one zip code to another, but FedEx's twist was to get things there overnight. FedEx had grabbed up nearly all the business jets that could do the job and put themselves in a position where they could not be easily replaced. As a result, FedEx is still a shipping powerhouse today.

As you are building your new habit of looking for changes in the community, focus on opportunities rather than the negative side of change. And keep in mind that even hard times create opportunities. With the social distancing practices during the COVID-19 pandemic, delivery services and online shopping—even for things like groceries—experienced unbelievable growth. In fact, most successful new businesses are slight adjustments to existing businesses. Uber took internet-based maps, smartphones, and cars (all of which previously existed) and combined them in a new way. The result was a multi-billion-dollar business using previously existing elements.

You'll do better if you stay within your knowledge base. Find more Scrabble letters and keep putting them together to spell new words—words that others aren't using yet because your niche doesn't exist yet or is underserved.

LOOKING FOR CHANGE SHOULD BE A LIFELONG HABIT

Change opens doors to new potential business opportunities, but looking for change shouldn't slow down after you launch. It will serve you as you create your new business, and it will further serve you by helping you pivot with industry changes in the future.

It is said that the older a person (or company or industry) is, the more they resist change. There are countless examples of how businesses that did not change with the times ran into big trouble. Popular restaurant chains like Bennigan's. Retailers like Montgomery Ward. Even leading-edge electronics companies like Palm, Inc., have gone bankrupt.

But paying attention to change and moving with the market has allowed for some impressive growth as well. Apple is an obvious example and they outlasted countless computer manufacturers. We've also done a number of pivots along the way with our company. For example, we started our pilot-training business with in-person classes taught on weekends. When a friend suggested that we put our training on video, we resisted at first because we thought our personal presence was required to get the job done. Later, when we did create training videos, at first we used them as a tool in our existing in-person training. Instead of talking through an entire training session while using an overhead projector, using our own videos in the classroom allowed us to relax a little as the day progressed. As we increasingly used those videos as a big part of our training, we had more energy at the end of the day to work with customers who needed extra help.

Later, we were able to actually sell complete courses on VHS tapes to clients all across the country. Those video courses, along with direct mail, allowed us to teach pilots throughout the country in their own dining rooms and living rooms.

As time went on, we pivoted from VHS video tapes to CDs and DVDs, and now online video course delivery. We even have our online video training available for download and use on mobile devices running on almost any current operating system. Little changes in technology over the years have allowed us to grow and change with the times.

When people ask us why we are still eating regularly after being in the same business for over four decades, we answer that it can be explained by two simple rules:

1. We have always solicited and been very responsive to customer feedback—this helps ensure that we are continuing to meet customer needs and wants.

2. We have worked very hard at keeping up with technology—this has helped us scale the business, make it easier for customers to buy, and make our aviation learning more accessible to learning pilots everywhere.

KEEP IT SIMPLE, LIVE WITHIN YOUR RESOURCES, AND EMBRACE YOUR NICHE

Keeping your early business plans simple and focusing on your niche allows you to do two very important things. First, you can stay on top of your entire effort and not waste time exploring tangents that take even more time and money before you can launch and start earning income. Second, simplicity allows you to self-describe what you're doing so your target market easily grasps your offering. Some people call it an "elevator pitch," because if you hop on an elevator and somebody asks what you do, you don't have time for a multi-paragraph explanation. Keep it simple. Consider that FedEx had a brilliant marketing slogan that let them self-describe in just one sentence: "When it absolutely, positively has to be there overnight."

One of the biggest mistakes new entrepreneurs make is that they over-extend themselves well beyond their resources because their passion(s) lead them to be overly optimistic and believe it can't fail. They think, *All I need is* [fill in the blank: car, truck, manufacturing plant, computer-server farm, etc.] *and I'll be successful.* And then when something unpredictable happens, and it will, everything crumbles and they're on the hook for big money. We'll talk later about other ways around big investments, but the main thing is to avoid large, up-front loans that are well beyond your ability to repay unless everything goes perfectly. When you take out a loan but haven't even tested your business model for viability with real transactions and paying customers, we call that putting your future in hock.

Despite your grand visions of how you can have clients across a broad spectrum of an industry, and your belief that you can deliver better than long-time industry players, you're much better off if you focus on delivering to a narrow niche and proving your successful concept first.

If you're in the United States and you see an airplane flying overhead, there's a 50 percent chance that the pilots have taken one or more classes from King Schools. But we didn't start out with a vision of teaching as many pilots as possible or as many courses as possible for all the various aviation certifications. We started with a narrow niche, and we grew. We taught classes ourselves, in person, in selected locations in the western half of the country. As technology improved and we went from teaching with overhead projectors to videos as a tool during in-person training to VHS courses available for sale via mail order, we grew intentionally and profitably at each step and always within our means. We never repeated the mistake of growth for its own sake by any means necessary, like we had made with franchising the lubrication business.

THE STRUGGLE CAN BE LONG AND HARD OR SHORT AND FUN

To an outsider looking at most any entrepreneur as they tackle their new business venture, the struggle looks long and hard. If you design a business where you don't have passion or enough Scrabble letters, your business will indeed be a hard struggle for you, and if we had to bet on it, we'd bet failure will result more often than not. But when you are immersed in a passion or something you think is fun, you set yourself up for success. And if we had to bet on it, we'd bet you will be successful.

The beautiful thing about following the guidelines we have set up for you so far is that you will not be over-extended financially in the early years, and you'll also have proof of the viability and profitability of your business idea by the time you begin to greatly expand.

UNIQUE AND PROTECTED, STRUCTURED TO SELL

We've talked quite a bit about finding a unique niche for your business because it keeps your personal focus narrow enough to manage, helps you describe what you do in simple, understandable terms so you can market more easily, and allows you to test the viability more simply. But there's another aspect of a narrow niche you should consider: Protected concepts. Patents or provisional patents, copyrights, and even trademarks can go a long way to keeping you protected from the competition.

One of your considerations should be to protect your business concept. You don't want your niche target market to see your potential competitors (usually longtime industry players) as an equal competitor to you. If you create a brilliant widget but without a patent, you're sure to invite competitors to make their own version and undercut your price, driving you out of business in no time. But a provisional patent ("patent pending") can give you some time to get out there in the market, and gives you the right, if needed, to sue copycats for stealing your patented design.

Niche safeguards don't have to be patents, though. They could be some other unique offering or maybe a personality. Training companies of all kinds capitalize on the credibility of their trainers and copyrights. Training course content is considered copyrighted material, especially if you include that © symbol in the training materials. Certain web software companies offer unique, copyrighted code that simplifies customer interactions online. Just consider your unique approach and how you might be able to best protect your offering so it can't be easily copied.

Another consideration to keep in mind: Selling your company should always be on your radar. You may want to keep things going just like they are until you retire, or you might want to move on to some new adventure after just a few years. Either way, you'll benefit by keeping your business in order so it's ready to sell if a great opportunity arises.

"Ready to sell" just means that you should keep accounting, inventory, and personnel policies, and customer and vendor lists in good order so you can easily sell your business without having to undergo months or years of educating others in order to do the handoff. You may have no intention of selling your business, but you never know what new possibility might be just around the corner.

TEST AND ANALYZE YOUR IDEA

Once you have an idea for a business, consider the early profit potential, but make sure the business meshes with your personality and that you will enjoy it. One without the other will not help you succeed. And keep in mind that only *you* know how you feel. Don't pay attention to others when you're considering how to feel about your business. Others may think they have your best interests in mind—they may even claim they know you better than you know yourself—but there's no way they can put aside their own personal doubts and values enough to get inside your head and know how *you* really feel about your business idea.

No business will provide you with all positives and no negatives, so you have to assign your values to the various aspects of your prospective business and decide what's best for you.

QUESTIONS AND PROMPTS TO HELP YOU DESIGN YOUR WINNER

Once you understand what goes into designing a winning business and why just following one of your passions or finding some niche isn't enough, the tools below can help you analyze opportunities and narrow your options so you can design your winner. You can use some or all of these questions and tools for your analysis. Go through the list and use those that make sense with your personal set of Scrabble letters and the marketplace.

You are looking for a way you can profitably and ethically help others gain something, save money, avoid trouble, or solve a problem at a price they are willing to pay.

Ask yourself these questions:

- What do you dislike about an area of interest to you? What can you improve?
- Do others who share your interest in that industry or community also dislike the same thing(s)?
- Can you improve in a way that eliminates that annoying thing? (When looking for those irritating things you could fix, listen when your friends complain, and pay close attention whenever they say, "They ought to . . .")
- Can you solve other people's problems?
- When there are big layoffs in a particular company or industry, can you provide services that make up for some of what was lost with the layoffs?
- Are there new industries or have there been big changes in existing industries?

- Is there some new invention that could use a companion new invention?

- Can you leverage a little-known invention to provide a special service?

- Are there any ways you can leverage an unexpected success, business, or lifestyle trend? (Such as leveraging Zoom or online meetings that exploded during the COVID-19 lockdowns.)

- Is there something that doesn't make sense?

- Can you practice creative imitation? (In other words, is there an industry player you could mimic but creatively improve each of their offerings by asking, "How could I do this better?")

- What skill could you master beyond the capabilities of anyone else in that field?

- How can you save someone a lot of time or money or effort? (FedEx delivers overnight and they charge a premium. Our lube trucks serviced fleet equipment at night—keeping the trucks productive during the daytime.)

- Can you introduce something to a new market that has never considered it before? (Liquid soap had been around industrial locations for years before someone offered it to consumers.)

- Are there any old fads you could resurrect?

- What success story could you borrow and twist to make it new and unique?

- Can you consider working for someone in the industry that interests you? (Don't go into competition with them but see what parallel opportunities exist.)

Also consider:

- Check with the Small Business Administration (SBA) to learn about trends and things people want.
- Consider 3D printing and small-volume, prototype-creation companies to make working versions of something you're considering creating.
- Visit trade shows and attend trade association meetings.
- If you have something patentable and you can afford to register a patent and create a few prototypes, consider online funding campaigns to underwrite your volume manufacturing costs.

Once you start to narrow your focus a bit, think about whether or not you're up to the challenge:

- Are you really equipped to do it? (No one is an overnight success. People can develop their talents over time, but you need to have enough talent, skill, or insight to be somewhat successful when you start.)
- Do you have the primary skills?
- Do you believe in the business?

- Do you have a history with the main subject of the business?
- Will you be interested in this business/industry in a few years?
- Are you comfortable with the lifestyle this business will require? (If travel is a big part of the business but you don't enjoy it, don't do it.)
- Could you redesign the business structure to fit your preferred lifestyle?
- Does your business match your self-image? (If you prefer wearing jeans and your job would require you to wear a suit all the time, that could be a deal-breaker.)
- Is the business trivial or important? (Stay away from trivial. You want to stay away from a business that gets dropped as soon as your customers' money gets just a little bit tight.)

Evaluate the business itself:

- If the business is successful, how profitable could it be in a few years?
- Are there any economies of scale? (Manufacturing can leverage this concept, because as demand grows and more product is produced, it's possible to reduce the cost of supplies and manufacturing.)
- Just be aware that there are some diseconomies of scale. (Some businesses can become less efficient and more

expensive as they grow. That tends to be true of service businesses.)

- How small is the smallest profitable unit of business?
- Can you finance future business growth from direct cash flow?
- Can you rent, lease, and subcontract some or all of your business so you minimize out-of-pocket investments? (Borrowing might be OK, but it's not a great idea because you must give up partial ownership of some assets to secure the loan.)
- Will you need outside stockholders to launch your business? (Stay away from selling stock as a startup, if you can, because you'll immediately have stockholders who are part owners, and they don't have your commitment or passion. Serving them can slow you down or sidetrack important plans. Once the business is large and growing, stockholders are okay.)
- Can your selling price be set high enough to make the business reasonably profitable in short order? (Along those lines, think hard before choosing to sell a commodity that people buy based on price alone. You need to have some special characteristic so you can charge more for it and so your competition cannot easily replicate your offering.)
- Does your business appeal to a special group?
- Is the end result (your product or service) difficult to obtain without you?

- What will it take to reach your target market? (What are your direct marketing, advertising, and publicity options?)
- Can you get the world behind you? (Is there a way to present yourself so you generate good will automatically? Consider how TOMS gives away a pair of shoes to a child in need whenever someone buys a pair for themselves.)
- Can success happen quickly?

Consider the competition:

- A little competition is a good thing—it demonstrates that there is a viable market and you must be thoughtful about your approach, quality, and value.
- A patent can help. So can custom packaging or some special twist with your offer.
- Could your business be sold to a competitor in the future?

YOUR SHORT LIST OF WINNERS AND THE RIGHT TIME TO LAUNCH

Going through the process of designing and analyzing your unique winner might take weeks or months, but don't keep pushing out your startup date indefinitely because of fear. You can eliminate fear. Be smart. Apply due diligence. Avoid risks.

HOW COME YOU ARE EATING REGULARLY?

People often ask us how it is we are doing well after over four decades in the same business. We answer that we follow these two simple rules:

1. We have always solicited customer feedback and been very responsive to it.
    - Our philosophy is that our business success is based on seeking out and taking care of the needs of our customers.
    - We won't know whether we are doing that unless we actively solicit customer feedback and respond to it.

2. We have kept up with changes in technology.
    - We started out giving live classes using <u>overhead projectors</u> (you put transparencies with the message on glass with a light underneath and mirrors projected the image onto the screen).
    - From there we went to <u>video cassettes,</u> which allowed us to vastly multiply the size of our audience because we could mail the courses out to learning pilots everywhere in the country—and even internationally.
    - Then we put the videos on computer <u>compact discs</u> (CDs).
    - Next, we put them on digital video discs (DVDs).
    - From there we put our courses <u>online.</u>
    - And then we developed apps to let folks take our courses <u>offline</u>

<u>on mobile devices</u> like smartphones and tablets.

All of this made our learning much more accessible, clear, and convenient.

Martha

4

TESTING YOUR CONCEPT FOR SUCCESS

You do, as you read this book, most likely by now, have a clear idea of a successful entrepreneurial mindset. You may also have a mental vision of what a business is and is not. It is our opinion that understanding these concepts will be a key element in the success of your own business.

BEFORE CREATING A VISION OF YOUR BUSINESS, YOU MUST UNDERSTAND WHAT YOUR BUSINESS IS NOT

Over the years, we have had quite a few visitors to the San Diego home office of King Schools. Students, friends of employees, and countless customers have had occasion to visit our office. Interestingly, a number of people who are not entrepreneurs (and even some budding entrepreneurs) have commented, based on looking at the King Schools business building, "You have a wonderful business here."

Ironically, that disappoints us.

We believe every entrepreneur needs to understand that our business, your business, and any business is *not* the building. It's not the equipment. It's not even the employees or the sales.

A business is the identification of a customer need or want that you can fulfill *profitably*.

THE SOLE AUTHORITY THAT SHOULD TALK YOU OUT OF YOUR BUSINESS IDEA (OR MAKE YOU ADJUST)

In Chapter Two, we emphasized the critical importance of following your passions as a path to a successful business. When you are following a passion, you'll put more in and get more out of your business. On the path of following your passions, it's important to not let well-meaning friends or family talk you out of your business idea. They don't know what you know, and they don't have exactly the same combination of passions you have.

However, beyond friends and family there is a single authority that actually should talk you out of your business idea if they tell you that your idea won't work. That authority is research.

Passion alone won't be enough to build your successful business. You have to research the marketplace and find out what needs or problems people have that you can solve for a profit. Research, or what we often call "testing," will keep you from throwing money at a business idea that you believe "should" work because it aligns with your passions and it's something people "should" want. That kind of "should" thinking has driven more entrepreneurs out of business than any competition ever has.

WHAT ARE YOU ACTUALLY TESTING?

Before you invest a lot of money, it would be wise to find out if you have identified a customer need or want that you can fulfill profitably. A lot of the tests and methods we describe below might appear to be descriptions of how to refine advertising for an existing business. While it's true that many of these testing concepts do work for improving the marketing and advertising for existing businesses, you can use the same tools to gauge market interest in your concept.

Depending on what your business will sell, one method to test whether people will buy it is to come up with a simplified or prototype version and see if people are willing to pay for it. For instance, before you invest in a full-scale restaurant, you could offer catering services. If you're going to sell online training, you can do a simple version of a class or course with a minimal investment in a rented room—like a hotel meeting room. The key is to get some kind of very simple version of your offering and start using the market-testing methods we describe to see if people are interested.

DON'T FALL IN LOVE WITH YOUR AMAZON VILLAGE

Years ago, we had some friends who had a background from Brazil and a real love of Brazilian food. They opened a Brazilian restaurant on a full-scale basis and were sure their concept would be a smash hit as soon as people had a chance to try the food. They called their restaurant "The Amazon Village" and they served delicious meat-filled turnovers they called "Marabas." Marabá is a municipality in the state of Pará, Brazil.

Unfortunately, we were just about the only customers who loved their Marabas. They waited and waited for customers to appear, and it just didn't happen. They kept putting in more and more money to keep the doors open, but the momentum never built up. Then they borrowed against their life insurance. Then they took out a second mortgage on their house. We encouraged them to test something else or change their restaurant plan, but they were so in love with their concept, they felt like any change would be untrue to their vision.

When they finally ran out of money and had to abandon the business, they had spent every bit of their savings. They had borrowed and put their future in hock. They sold their restaurant equipment to another company that came into the very same location and opened a seafood restaurant called "The Maine Thing." Within two weeks, there was a line out the door of people waiting to get in and enjoy the new seafood restaurant.

The very same location with the very same restaurant equipment was successful because they offered a different concept and menu. If only our friends had made changes instead of borrowing and dumping all their money into a business that wasn't working, hoping that people would eventually "catch on."

If our friends had tested something else, and paid attention to the feedback, they could have changed their menu or changed their concept and been successful. But they just stuck with the concept they loved. They stuck with their passion and stubbornly refused to pay attention to the automatic research results of not enough paying customers.

OUR EARLY RESEARCH

Our earliest research happened before there was a King Schools, while we were instructors working for an aviation training company called Ross Ground School. At the time, we were enjoying flying and teaching others the knowledge they needed to fly (called "ground school"), and we weren't really itching to start a new business. We didn't deliberately set out to learn how to start a business from the competition.

At Ross Ground School, we recognized that the most packed classes were usually in towns where there wasn't a large city or large airport for hundreds of miles. In a big metropolis, finding a flight school that also runs a ground school is no problem. But finding a flight school in small towns west of the Mississippi was considerably harder. Whenever we'd teach our weekend ground-school class in one of those less-populated locations, we would hear from students that a 300-mile drive to take our class was not out of the question. Nevertheless, Ross Ground School didn't focus on the locations with the biggest classes. They went to cities big and small.

We were enjoying teaching and weren't planning on becoming our employer's competition, but they made a mistake that resulted in their going out of business, and that inspired us to start ours. Ironically, they went under because they had the same kind of bad business goal that helped put our oil-and-lube business under. Their mistake was what we refer to as "defective goal setting." We'd had a goal of fifty franchisees nationwide. Ross Ground School had a goal of hiring ten sets of traveling ground instructors. In each case, the word "profitable" was not included. Ross was able to hire those instructors, but they hadn't considered whether there was enough potential at all those locations to employ the instructors profitably.

As soon as Ross Ground School let us know they were going out of business, we stepped into our own venture. Out of necessity we had a very small budget. We had some posters printed so we could advertise a class we planned to do and ask potential customers to call to sign up for our class. Our testing consisted of placing posters in aviation service businesses at smaller airports near where we lived. We paid the businesses a small percentage for the use of their facilities to conduct our classes. The advantage to the local businesses, in addition to a small income, was that we brought aviation customers into their facilities. The classes were small, but profitable.

Each profitable class gave us the cash we needed to advertise the next class. Soon we were able to keep advertising classes continually. After we had built up some momentum, we looked for other ways to market. We started renting hotel meeting rooms and arranging classes in cities with the characteristics we thought would support our classes. We developed a direct-mail piece and sent it to pilots and prospective pilots within driving distance of the classes. We used postal mailing lists of pilots available at that time from the Federal Aviation Administration (FAA). We didn't have enough money to do big mailings and schedule lots of classes, so we had to have a profitable class before we could advertise the next one. Each successful class funded the next class, and so on. And each successful class showed us where we could profitably return.

The important takeaway isn't the specific tools we used—the lesson is that it's important to test before you start and always keep testing during the entire life of your business.

These days, due to all the digital alternatives, it's less likely that ground-school courses would have much success using posters for market research, and the FAA mailing lists aren't even available anymore. But there are avenues that are faster and more precise, like the internet and email, that allow us to continue to test marketing ideas.

WORKING FOR A COMPETITOR

Maybe most significantly, our very first, incredibly valuable source of market research was Ross Ground School. If you can go to work for someone in a similar business so you can learn about the marketplace, you can learn practically all the ins and outs of the industry. If you are careful, you can do it very ethically.

For example, going into direct competition in the same marketplace would be unethical and would leave your ex-employer feeling unfairly treated. Going after current clients whom you met because of your job would also be unfair. In some states, employers can have you sign a noncompete agreement, so it could be illegal for you to work for a competitor or as a direct competitor (laws on this vary from state to state). But it is possible for you to do it and be beyond reproach and completely forthcoming. One key is to tell your employer what your long-term plans are.

A good example would be if you got a job in a restaurant. You could learn about health department regulations, food supplier relationships, inventory management, and all kinds of things that go into running a successful restaurant. Most successful restaurants and restaurant chains were started by somebody who had worked in a restaurant before. It's incredibly rare that someone would start a restaurant without some previous experience in the business.

Popular restaurants actually expect that some of their employees will go to work at another restaurant or will start their own. But starting a submarine sandwich shop in a strip mall right across the street from the sub shop where you had been working for a year, with similar sandwich offerings, would leave your former employer feeling unfairly treated. Doing it in a different section of town or miles away with a totally different menu would be no problem.

Another possibility is to work for a parallel business that's similar to what you want to do, but is not in direct competition. You could go to work for an auto parts store before you start your auto repair shop. You could work for an auto repair shop before opening up a body shop.

Yet another possibility is to work in the kind of business you'd like to own, but do it in a non-competitive geographic location where there aren't overlapping marketplaces. If your planned bakery or flower shop is a two-hour drive from where you used to work, that shouldn't be a problem.

High-tech jobs have similar limitations and opportunities, though they aren't usually tied to geography. You could be a programmer or social media marketer for a company and then step out on your own, as long as you don't take business or customers from your former employer.

MODERN RESEARCH—KEYWORDS CAN INDICATE AUDIENCE INTEREST

The internet—and more specifically, social media, search engines, and email—has opened up huge test-marketing opportunities for entrepreneurs and, in most cases, at very affordable prices compared to traditional advertising. Plus, you get quick results. You don't have to buy a big ad for a magazine's full circulation and then wait weeks or months for the magazine to be printed and the mail service to deliver it before you start getting feedback.

The internet lets you do the same kind of thing as magazine ads much more quickly, with a much lower budget, and with far greater precision. For example, you can design a simple ad or offer and pay Google or Facebook or YouTube or Instagram to run your ad—either nationally, or (more cheaply) geo-targeted to a specific small area. Then you can see exactly how many people respond to that ad. You can cap your investment so you never run over budget. And you can have several different types of ads running at the same time.

Digital marketing is a rapidly evolving field. As an entrepreneur, you will want to learn as much as you can on the subject.

SMART STRATEGIES FOR ALL-MARKET TESTING

You will find listed below some useful strategies and approaches that we used in the early days of our marketing that are still universally important today.

Response-advertising basics:

- Make a clear and definite offer.
- Include all the information necessary to make a decision.
- Give the motivation to take action now.
- Provide an easy means of response.

Learning from direct marketing:

- Track your response.
- Measure your outcome.
- Respond to what you learn.

ALWAYS SPLIT-TEST YOUR OFFERS, AND DON'T TEST WHISPERS

By definition, split-testing (often called A/B testing) is where you send out an advertisement or offer to a target market and you have two or more versions of the ad. You split the list in half and send one version to each half, then track the responses to see which ad or offer attracted more response and/or made more sales. Around King Schools, you'll hear staff talking about A/B testing all the time, because we want to know if ad A or ad B works better.

If you create an ad and then change *anything* in the ad and send the changed version to a different list in that same target market, that's considered "split-testing." It's possible to change nuanced elements like the color or font of the headline or a few words in the body copy, but you will get far more valuable information by testing substantial things rather than subtle changes. It has often been said, "Don't test whispers."

The most worthwhile changes for split-testing tend to be based on an adjustment to the offer. Experienced direct marketers consider it works best when you send the two versions of your offer to every other user on a particular list, rather than using something like geography or age of the customer record to make your splits.

Another valuable thing to test is the results from one list versus another: for example, a list you bought from a trade group compared to a list from an industry website. Of course, you should measure the effectiveness of each of your lists.

Once we have a winner at King Schools, we'll set up more and more A/B tests and continue to see which gets the best response. We'll change things like the price or the structure of the offer, the guarantee, an included bonus, or something else of significance that changes the value proposition. Whichever version produces the best result becomes our new "control," meaning the version we test against the next time. It's a continual process of slow but steady improvement.

Because digital ad offers can be changed for practically zero added cost, and because tracking is incredibly simple and precise, there's no reason to ever put out a single offer with no split test. The results will always tell you something about your marketing effectiveness, and A/B tests are essentially free research.

SEARCH ENGINE OPTIMIZATION (SEO) HELPS TOO

How your company and your offers show up in internet search engines is a result of constantly changing algorithms used by search engines. If you can use web traffic to test your business concepts or see if there's actually a market out there, an understanding of how to use SEO can be helpful.

Search engine companies have two primary goals. First, they want to help users find resources on the web that match what they say they're looking for while ranking available resources by value. Second, they want to leverage those searches to drive users to businesses that pay the search engine companies to get found.

Search engine companies don't ever reveal all the items that will help a company rank high in organic search results (unpaid), but some best practices allow you to optimize your content for how search engines sort and rank content. This is called search engine optimization (SEO). Most web content creators are well aware of common best practices for SEO, but all optimization is not created equal.

If you have a nice big budget and you want to pay search engine companies (like Google) for help, you can bid on keywords to drive traffic to your site and/or offer. That's called "pay per click" (PPC). If you pay for keywords as part of your advertising, it might cost you $5 or $20 each time a search engine user clicks on a keyword you paid for, which redirects them to your website. That is often too expensive for most businesses and definitely for most startups.

However, if you can find out what some of the expensive keywords are in your industry or community, you can weave those words into your web page articles, your offer descriptions, and your video descriptions. The more you are able to incorporate popular search terms into your content, the more likely you will be found in searches. Of course, the use of those words needs to be in proper context. You can't just create pages with a particular word used again and again, or hide keywords in the code of your web page for search engines to find while remaining invisible to site visitors. That's considered "cheating" by the search engines, which are seeking to maintain a system that serves the users well.

BE QUALITY

The best way to demonstrate that you are serving your customers well is to create quality content. If your content is an instructional video or a blog post, you will impress the system the best with quality original content. Hosting your content on a reliable web server that follows all the current regulations on internet privacy and security is important, as is using relevant terms throughout your article or in your video description. Later, as you can afford it, hire web professionals with SEO experience in your field to help you further refine and update your content to get even better search results.

AUTHENTICITY WORKS

On the web, just like so many other aspects of business, authenticity pays. When everything you do is trustworthy and consistent with industry standards, you get better results. Generating web traffic based on sketchy practices will get you de-listed, and that's far worse than a low listing.

For example, buying followers on social media to boost your "credibility" is a trick that quite a few YouTubers and social media "influencers" have tried in order to appear to have a large audience. They attempt to leverage that apparent large following to charge big money for testimonials and advertising on their platform or channel. As soon as companies do a little research and find that a substantial number of followers are from questionable sources, like 50,000 followers from Taiwan who follow an English-speaking computer software reviewer, they lose credibility. Frequently, the platforms themselves (YouTube, Facebook, Instagram, etc.) discover the illegitimate followers and delete them, causing someone's apparent popularity to disappear overnight.

There are even things most of us wouldn't think of as cheating but that platform owners say is against their policy, and that can reduce the reach of users who break their rules. For example, videos that get lots of "likes" or "shares" will be made more visible by the platform managers, so people ask for likes and shares. However, saying "please like and share this video" out loud on a video posted on social media or YouTube can cause the automatic algorithms to reduce the reach of that video.

The bottom line is that the platforms want to eliminate any ways people can easily rank higher or be found more easily, other than through direct payment. Facebook, YouTube, Instagram, and others want a completely level playing field so they can sell increased visibility and make money. Trying to cheat the system will risk getting you shut down or demoted to greatly reduced visibility.

BEST PRACTICES FOR TESTING: GREAT CONTENT AND FREE STUFF

The best approach to testing ads—and even unpaid content like blog posts and articles or free videos—is to create good content and label it properly. The other thing is to give something away for free—and that free thing doesn't even have to cost you anything. It could be information, training, or a downloadable PDF guide of some kind. This is especially worthwhile if you're testing out a new business idea to see if people might be interested.

WHY FREE STUFF WORKS

People do business more quickly and comfortably when they know, like, and trust a person or company. Someone is much more likely to buy from a company they've heard of than some random company that pops up from a Google search. At King Schools, we have a number of free video courses we offer to potential customers as well as current clients. These free courses help people get to know us and our teaching style, which increases the chances they will think about King Schools when they are looking for additional training. Also, our free courses trigger "the law of reciprocity."

THE LAW OF RECIPROCITY

If a friend of yours ever picked up the tab at lunch, it's likely that you made the effort to get the check next time and return the favor. When somebody shares something nice about you or your business on social media, you might feel thankful enough that you go out of your way to say something nice about them. If a friend invites you to a party, you'll probably feel obligated to invite them to a party you're throwing too.

It's human nature to remember a favor we appreciate, and we feel compelled to return that favor.

There's an online auto parts retailer that puts out countless free, quality instructional videos about doing various simple repairs on all kinds of cars and trucks. These are simple videos that cover installations and repairs that are easy enough that home mechanics will likely try to do the repair themselves. That way, when the consumer combs through YouTube to figure out how to install a window motor on their particular model of car, they end up feeling obligated to buy the part from the company that put out the free training.

DON'T ASK FOR TOO MUCH AND DON'T BE PUSHY!

Free stuff to attract attention is not new to the web. It's practically standard operating procedure to put out some sort of free, information-packed video and then get people to "just click the link below" to get access to a free class. The problem that arises is when the free class requires that you give up your email address *and* complete a mini-survey *and* watch a "short" commercial, just to see the free content. And then the problem is compounded when the "free" class holds back some part of vital information that should have been in the class, and offers it for a one-time-payment of "just" $7. A lot of times, if you jump in for the $7 purchase, they give you a second one-time-offer (OTO) to some monster upgrade that's $49 or $997. That experience leaves the customer feeling betrayed and diminishes loyalty.

Infomercials on late-night TV used to sucker people into buying, but today they're considered a joke and only sell a fraction of what they once did. Likewise, consumers today hate the free offer with a second one-time-offer (OTO) and built-in upsell. A few people still do it but it doesn't work very well anymore, and it builds an audience of distrusting, annoyed people who actually could have become customers if you had treated them well.

But wait! Didn't we just say we offer free courses?

Yes, we do. But it's all about a small, simple ask and no pushy upsell sales pitch. All we ask for is an email address and then we let people take the class. The course has true value and there's no upsell at the end of the course. We don't have any one-time-offers or limited-time-offers that will disappear in the next twenty-four hours.

Ultimately, we do reach out to students of the free courses, but it's not overwhelming or pushy and we never do the OTO or limited-time hard sales push. Our offers are low-key and consistent with what customers have expressed an interest in. The idea is to preserve the element of trust.

THE VALUE WE GOT FROM A
DIRECT MARKETING SEMINAR

Martha thought we should go to a direct marketing seminar. I thought that at around $500 (in 1983) for a couple of days, it was too expensive. Martha told me about all the things she thought she'd learn and said, "I am going to go."

I stayed home. When she came back, she said, "I learned something very interesting. They said that if you mail a solicitation to a certain group and it is successful, and if you can afford a 30 percent drop in sales, you can mail the exact mailer to the same group a month later and capture 70 percent of the sales you had the previous month."

We had been mailing solicitations to flight instructors, but after we had mailed to the entire national list of flight instructors we quit mailing to them. Based on what Martha learned at the seminar, we were able to resume mailing profitably to this list. We made a lot more money from sales to flight instructors that year, and I became a believer in direct marketing seminars.

John

CHAPTER

5

MANAGING YOUR RISK

Y** ou will, as an entrepreneur, have to come to terms with risk. Just as with many activities, including the flying we enjoy so much, business has associated risks. Success in either endeavor requires identifying risks and figuring out how to mitigate them. We are sad to have to tell you we have failed at risk management in each endeavor— we have had an airplane crash and a business bankruptcy.

Each experience has made us more thoughtful about managing the associated risks. Consequently, we have developed aviation risk-management courses in our aviation education business and this chapter will, we hope, provide valuable risk-management tools for entrepreneurs.[1]

---

[1] If you would like to learn more about our airplane crash and aviation risk management, go to https://kingschools.com/how-to-avoid-unwanted-adventure.

LIFE AND DEATH VS. BROKE AND NOT BROKE — IT'S ALL ABOUT MANAGING RISK

You will be interested to know that there are many similarities between and aviation and business risk management. As we mentioned, the goal in each is to identify and mitigate risks on the way to accomplishing your goal. One of the problems regarding the discussion of risk management in the flying community is that many people have over-simplified the decisions by diminishing the complex process of flying to a "go/no-go" decision. The problem with that is that once a decision is made to "go," there is a tendency to think that the risk-management process is over. The result is that many risks, especially those that come along later, are ignored rather than managed.

In both aviation and business, good risk management is an ongoing process of conducting surveillance for risks and then making changes to mitigate those risks. In aviation, we use a mnemonic as a tool to aid in the process, and the same tool can be helpful in business. That tool is C-CARE.

The first C stands for "changes." As soon as you get airborne or start in business, everything you planned beforehand starts changing. For instance, in an airplane, once you start flying your fuel supply starts decreasing. As time passes, the pilot becomes more fatigued. the airplane flies over changing terrain, and the weather changes. Likewise, in early business operations it is not unusual for your cash supply (the equivalent of fuel) to start decreasing due to expenses that exceed revenue.

The next C stands for "consequences." That prompts you to think about the consequences of all the changes you have identified.

The A in CARE prompts you to think about how the alternative courses of action available to you are fewer or different as a result of the changes. In an airplane, as fuel is consumed, the geographic circle of alternatives gets smaller. In business, as cash is consumed, your circle of alternatives likewise gets smaller.

The R in CARE stands for "reality." You need to deal with things as they really are, not as you planned them to be. Both pilots and entrepreneurs tend to refuse to recognize changes they don't like.

Pilots have two very valuable risk-management sayings that can help keep you out of trouble in both aviation and business:

- Deal with things as they really are, not as you planned them to be.
- When things change, change your plan.

The solution is to identify problems when they happen and address them. Over-optimism about the future of your business can blind you to big financial problems until it's too late.

The E in CARE stands for "external pressures." We think of them as both external and internal (self-generated) pressures. It prompts pilots and entrepreneurs to think about the pressures that make them ignore changes and risks. For either a pilot or an entrepreneur, the requirement to change plans could cause a loss of face. That pressure to avoid losing face can result in denial and subsequent disaster if you do not deal with the change.

RISKS IN BUSINESS

Just as our airplane crash made us much more thoughtful about aviation risk management, our bankruptcy made us much more thoughtful about business risk management.

The thoughts below will help you see and understand business risks. We will also discuss business pitfalls and how to avoid them.

You Make Money in Business by Managing Risks, Not by Courting Risks

Most business ideas don't work as originally planned, but that doesn't mean you shouldn't try your business idea. Because many ideas don't work as first envisioned, testing becomes very important. Most successful entrepreneurs start by testing out some of their initial ideas, failing a few times in a small way, refining their ideas, testing again, and finally nailing things down with a winner. Similarly, before landing a helicopter in a remote area, pilots are taught to conduct a "high reconnaissance" followed by a "low reconnaissance." The idea is to inspect the landing area at several different altitudes before committing to a riskier full approach and landing.

In business, you don't always need a complete, fully staffed, fully functioning business to test your business idea. Many times there are ways to test the concept by offering a partial version of the bigger business plan. As we mentioned in Chapter Four, you can test a restaurant concept by offering catering before launching a location-based restaurant. A very successful restaurant near Savannah, Georgia, started as a food truck that visited various locations. They evolved to a fixed-location food truck and eventually built their actual restaurant at their successful food truck location.

In modern times, you can test countless businesses in a very affordable way by using the internet to scout potential target clients and see if the proposed concept will work. Testing usually includes targeted advertisements, followed by continuous refinement of the concept until there is a profitable formula. That is the foundation on which to build your business.

Avoid Long-Term Commitments and Stay Flexible

All businesses have a life cycle. Make sure that the product or service you're offering has a reasonable future for growth. In the '80s, going into the designer home TV antenna business while cable TV is exploding is a bad idea. With any new concept, you will want to ask yourself whether your potential market is expanding or contracting.

Don't Commit to Your Concept before It Is Proven

You may be captivated by a particular cuisine because you loved it while living in a foreign country, but if there isn't a sufficient interest in what you're offering based on the sign outside your restaurant, you won't get enough people to come inside and try the food so you can pay the bills. It would be wise to test the local interest in that cuisine before you commit your future to it in a long-term business.

Structure to Avoid Disaster

People who have made a lot of money in business have usually done so by being stingy and cautious. There's no question that you'll need to spend money, but it's best to do so from a mindset of stinginess. When you spend too quickly and become starved for cash, you have fewer alternatives and management becomes more difficult. As a result, the business begins to consume you and you make decisions based on saving cash rather than long-term profit. Be tight and stay cash-positive and you'll maintain your alternatives.

Too Many Business Owners Want to "Operate in Style"

Once things start to get going, some entrepreneurs get caught up in what they perceive is the lifestyle of a successful business owner, and they spend too much on personal luxuries to show they are successful—increasing the risk of running out of cash.

Lifestyle choice has been the downfall of many proud business owners. They don't want to live in a particular neighborhood or drive a particular car because they feel they have had enough business success to move past that less-expensive house or car. And when the business starts losing money, they don't cut personal luxuries until it's too late.

Keeping sufficient cash to be agile is key. Structure your business so that if things don't work out the way you planned, you can make the required changes to move toward profitability or, if necessary, just cease doing business without a financial disaster.

Small Businesses Have an Advantage over the Big Guys

One of the advantages small businesses have over large businesses is the flexibility to change quickly. Keep that flexibility and the increased alternatives it provides by not committing to any non-critical fixed expenses. Don't make long-term commitments to fixed costs until you prove long-term potential.

Don't Build Your House on Rented Land

There are all kinds of ways people are reaching customers these days, like using social media and internet services—which they don't own. It's fine to use those platforms for advertising, but your goal should always be to own your own customer lists as soon as you can. A business that is entirely based on a YouTube channel or a Facebook group is controlled by YouTube or Facebook. As a result, they can put you completely out of business with a single change in policy or their viewing algorithms. As soon as possible, start owning your own website and customer email, address, and phone lists.

Only Borrow against Assets

Unless there's an asset available to cover the loan, borrowing money to cover expenses before your revenue is established creates a risk of owing money with no way to pay it back. If things get tough, the loan becomes a burden on the business and adds to your problems. Assets depreciate, so don't fool yourself by believing an asset is worth what you paid for it. An asset is only worth what you can sell it for.

Borrowing money to keep a losing business open is a risky proposition—it could just prolong your problems. You'll be much happier if you can figure out a way to generate positive cash flow from the business instead of by borrowing—it is the best, least-risky way to keep your business open.

Having a policy of paying for expenses in cash generates a discipline of keeping expenses in control. This policy will serve you very well in the long run as an entrepreneur, and will help you set your investment limits. If you want to avoid bankruptcy, you will want to decide in advance how much you can afford to invest or lose in a business, and stop when you hit that limit. Real-world goal posts like this will help promote a discipline of keeping expenses in line with revenues.

WHEN IT'S TIME TO CUT

Don't Lose by Default

A discipline of paying attention to your income and expenses—and having strict rules in place to make expense cuts before losses pile up—will serve you well in any business. Remember that failing to actively make a decision means you are still making a decision. You are just making it by default instead of thoughtfully.

Cut Expenses in Time

The habit of stopping the loss of money by quickly cutting expenses can save your business when hard times come. You may feel bad about having to cut staff or reduce other precious resources that cost you money, but waiting to make those cuts puts you at much greater risk of losing your business entirely.

All businesses make money by making sales, so it's natural to think that spending more energy and effort on the sales process is the first thing to do when you start losing money. It's actually the second thing.

When times get tough, it is wise to cut expenses first because you have more control over expenses and can get quicker results. That will tip the bank balance more quickly in your favor and give you a bigger window of opportunity to push for more sales.

AVOID PITFALLS

Finally, here are a few concepts you should consider as you're planning your entrepreneurial venture:

Avoid guaranteeing a loan as your contribution to a partnership. You may very well benefit from a partnership in your new business, but you need to apply the same level of risk mitigation to aspects of the partnership business that you would in a sole proprietorship. You never want to be on the hook for someone else's financial decisions or shortcomings.

You may want to consider that selling stock is a disadvantage. You are 100 percent accountable to your investors. That means that even if they don't have decision-making authority, you still need to keep them informed and consider their input seriously. That takes extra time and energy you likely may not have. Beyond that, you need an attorney to sell stock correctly, and that is a cost in and of itself.

SEVEN KEYS TO RISK MANAGEMENT

1. *Start out with expenses so low that you start your business profitably right out of the gate—and stay that way.*

A business without profit isn't a business. If your business idea needs to start out big in order to be able to have enough volume to generate a profit, or be whatever your vision is, you need to rework things until you figure out how to start profitably and small.

2. Be jealous of expenses.

Every dollar you spend on expenses is one that doesn't go into your pocket. Dreaming big puts too many beginning entrepreneurs in the mindset that they need to build an empire instead of an income. If you don't structure your business to deliver income first, you'll never get to the empire. A profitable business is far more important than a big business.

3. Don't try to impress people with trappings.

There may come a time, after you've been successful in business for a while and you have substantial savings and a solid, steady profit, when you can afford those lifestyle trimmings, but you shouldn't do that when you're just getting started.

4. Hire only when necessary.

Almost always, the largest single investment in most businesses is employees. If you think you need to hire someone, brainstorm all the alternatives first. As soon as you hire someone, you have all the management, supervision, and accounting problems that go along with having employees. Additionally, there is always some risk of having employees steal from you.

5. Subcontracting sets costs.

It is a good idea to subcontract work whenever you can. This sets the cost and converts costs from fixed to variable, since a variable cost is an expense that changes in proportion to production. Additionally, subcontractors are already set up in business and can get started on the job more quickly than you could, either by yourself or by hiring new employees.

For example, using an answering service instead of a receptionist is quicker and requires less commitment. Despite the general belief that there is no such thing as a good answering service, if you look around enough and pay appropriately, you'll find exactly what you need. If you are willing to pay a little extra, you can get them to provide specialized services adapted to your own business. Current technology allows those answering your business phone to work from their home or even in another country, and they can easily transfer calls or messages to you as necessary.

6. Work from your own home.
Even if you think you need an office, maybe you don't. Or maybe you can get by with a one- or two-person office with additional staffers working from home, and they can live anywhere in the country. Most people fully understand this possibility, and remote video meetings and quick access to shared group resources online (popularized during the COVID-19 pandemic due to government restrictions and the shift to working from home) makes the process much smoother. As meetings are needed, you can choose to meet up in countless locations, even if you don't maintain a small office.

7. Use part-time specialists.
People providing any one of dozens of services could be specialists who

work with you part time. Consider this for web development, social media presence, bookkeeping, and video production, among others. You get the benefit of a full-time expert, but only when you need them. And you can usually work out a reduced cost for their services based on their recurring visits and regular income for them.

WE TEACH WHAT WE KNOW AND BELIEVE

You will observe that we are suggesting a somewhat conservative approach to entrepreneurship. We believe in managing risk. You don't have to do it our way; in fact, many people have been successful after taking huge risks. Likewise, pilots have gotten by after taking huge risks as well. It's just that in both cases, we believe the odds are much more in your favor if you conduct risk surveillance, identify risks, and mitigate them.

Likewise, companies have gone years without making a profit and become very big and very successful in the process. Our approach of starting small, getting profitable soon, and growing while profitable is not the only way of doing it. You can start big on borrowed and invested money with a concept that starting big is best, and then sell lots of stock before you are even profitable. Uber is a case in point. That approach takes different skills and connections than the approach we are suggesting. We recommend our approach because we think it can work broadly, is the most likely route to success, and will benefit society well.

We teach pilots the knowledge to fly. We teach entrepreneurs how to be successful in business. We teach both groups how to manage risk. In business, we don't teach how to start big with no profit, get big investors, and eventually hope that your big business can become profitable. We don't teach the Uber approach to business. They went BIG and went public, seeking investors, and the millions rolled in. After years in business, the company only reported its first quarterly profit in November 2021.

A number of companies started with a big push to gain market share and lost money for years, then tipped the scales to a profitable business years later. Amazon comes to mind. But you won't find us suggesting that this is a good approach to starting a business, because while the success stories are great, this tactic has far too many opportunities for failure. There is a tendency to remember only the big success stories and not the thousands of failures and bankrupt broken dreams.

CHAPTER

6

REFINING YOUR BUSINESS PLAN

You understand by now how important it is for you to do what you love—it turns work into fun. We have always enjoyed teaching and we have had a habit of combining our passion for teaching with some other passion we had. Over the years, we have taught courses that are consistent with these other passions. The majority of our video and in-person courses have to do with flying. For instance, we had a course for ham radio operators (amateurs) when we were involved in that passion. Most significantly to the purpose of this book, we have offered courses on cassettes, DVDs, in print, and in person to help people along their entrepreneurial path. Throughout our entrepreneurial course materials, we discussed the importance of business plans and we provided some suggestions about what should be included in a business plan.

The most important business planning we have ever done was when we were starting our ground-school business. We sat down in a bedroom converted to an office with some notebook paper and talked with each other about what we wanted out of life. We set goals for the type of work we wanted to do, for the amount of money we wanted to make, and for the influence we wanted to have on the aviation community.

We didn't refer often to these notes, but they were in the back of our minds for decades afterwards. What is most fascinating is that not only did we meet those goals, we exceeded the income goals—which seemed outrageous and impossible when we originally discussed them.

WHEN FORMAL BUSINESS PLANNING CAN BE VALUABLE

A business plan is a valuable tool to help you improve your understanding of important aspects of your business.

Manage Your Costs

What will it cost to create the product or service you want to sell? What will it cost to get the word out about your offering? What expenses will you incur in helping clients? Can you use your currently owned car and computer and residence as a means of transportation, communication, bookkeeping, and location?

Understand the Government's Role

Does the business you're stepping into have any government regulations to which you must conform? Do you need to get any kind of license to legally deliver your product or service? This could be as simple as a business or professional license. There might be a state or federal bureau that regulates people doing your kind of business, and you may have to take some sort of test. You might be able to start testing the sales of your product or service as just an individual before securing a business license and/or forming a company. That works for many kinds of services like computer programming or selling a trinket online, but it won't work if your product is something that's especially regulated, like legal services, supplements, or food.

Understand the Industry Standards

Does your product or service need to meet industry standards in order to be available for legal sale?

Get Any Needed Credentials

Do you need to be a certified expert who has passed a test before you can legally sell your products or services? Hair stylists, CPAs, and flight instructors all need to meet regulatory requirements before they can legally offer their services. Do you know all the necessary certifications you'll need?

Overall, you need to really know the industry you're entering. You need to know about trade groups, government regulations, legal requirements, necessary insurance coverages, and what costs are involved with delivering your goods or services to the market. If you find yourself saying "I'm not sure" about any of the potential costs, it's worth jotting down your questions and investigating.

Make a Little Money

By the time you're actually launching a business, you need to be past the first phases of testing to see if people are willing to exchange their hard-earned money for what you're selling. Don't worry about logos. Don't worry about a retail location. Don't even worry about your business name until you've got proof that people will pay for what you want to sell. People buy products or services. They don't buy business names or logos.

NAME YOUR BUSINESS

Early in launching your business, you need to come up with a name. While having a good, functional business name is critical, following smart guidelines for naming your business will yield different kinds of results for different entrepreneurs. Be sure to check on city, county, and state business regulations so you follow guidelines about legally registering a fictitious name for your business. That used to require placing an ad in a local newspaper in many parts of the country, but these days it may simply require registering with a county clerk, city hall, or some other official. Check with your local government (e.g., city hall) and they'll be able to tell you.

Your business name should play to your audience, and that may not only be your customers. Do you need a high-tech or solid-sounding corporation name to impress suppliers in the technology fields? Consider all the audiences that may need to notice and remember your company name.

Use a Unique Name

Obviously, something like "Smith Lawn Care" is very likely taken and probably a business name in more than one state. A quick Google search of this random example yielded hundreds of lawn care and tree services with a similar or identical name in numerous states. The last thing you want to do is make it hard to find you with a quick Google search. If you don't stand out from the crowd, prospective clients might find a lot of your competitors instead.

Your first or last name might make sense to include in your business name, but it might not. A company name that doesn't feature the name of the founder might seem bigger than something with your last name in the mix—many small "mom and pop" businesses feature a surname as part of the name. If you plan to sell your business at some point in the future, would it be more or less valuable with your name still attached? Then when you do sell the business, if the new owners run the company into the ground or start doing something unethical, how will you feel about your name being attached to that company?

A Descriptive Name Could Be Good or Bad

If the description locks you into a technology or a concept, it could limit future growth, but for some businesses it could be helpful. A name like "Renee's" could be anything, so calling a business "Renee's Southern Kitchen" makes a lot more sense. But descriptive names have made for some rough patches for some businesses in the past. We remember when Motel 6 started as a place where rooms were six dollars per night. Sure, it made sense in the beginning, and they built a big motel chain as a result. But they also had many negative customer interactions when their rates had to move up with inflation. Over the years, they kept expressing their increasing rates with ".66" at the end of the price ($79.66, etc.) before abandoning the "6" connection in their pricing altogether.

Don't Tie Your Name to Technology That Will Evolve

In the same way that the name Motel 6 trapped a motel chain into a price-point perception, we have considered and rejected company names that would tie us to a specific technological perception. Our approach has always been to tie our company name to *what* we deliver, not *how*.

Our original business name was "King Accelerated Ground Schools." This was descriptive because aspiring pilots knew what "accelerated ground school" meant. Most competitive ground schools were taught over a period of six to eight weeks, and ours was taught on a single weekend. Later, as we added more courses and started delivering course content on VHS tapes, some staffers pushed us to name our company "King Video." Not only did that exclude the in-person classes we continued to teach, it sounded like we would be in the business of videotaping, not delivering aviation training. When we finally did change the name of our company, we had very good recognition in the industry, and simplifying the name to "King Schools" was what we decided to do.

Check the Internet

Once you come up with a name for your business, you should use Google to see if the name is already in use. The last thing you'll want to do is start a business and head to the county clerk's office to register it, only to discover that the name is already taken. Additionally, if your business name is very similar to others providing the same services, potential customers might be looking for you but find your competition instead.

In the end, your company name matters. Plan your name for now at launch, and for the future. Be sure it is unique. Keep it simple so it is easily remembered. If a descriptive name would help, weave that into your naming process. And register the fictitious name as required by local and state laws.

DEVELOP YOUR LOGO

You don't need a logo to start your business or during your early business-development testing and start-up phase. A logo won't help you find a customer need or want that you can fulfill profitably. Your logo should only be on your agenda *after* initial testing of the business idea. Once you start down the path to the early days of launching a full-fledged business, that's when you should get a logo.

Good logos are big, bold, and simple.

USE REMUS

Beyond that, we like the acronym REMUS for five other characteristics. Your logo should be:

- Relevant to your business
- Engaging to the target market
- Memorable
- Unexpected
- Simple

In the early days of King Schools, our logo included a plotter that pilots used on sectional charts to measure direction and distance when planning a trip or navigating in the air. It was a tool that helped you get where you wanted to go in your airplane, so using it in our logo made perfect sense to us. Pilots certainly recognized it, so it wasn't a bad logo—it just wasn't simple. Over time, though, we decided that the logo would have to change, partly because almost nobody uses plotters like that anymore. But our bigger reason for updating the logo was to better apply the REMUS standard, especially the part about keeping the logo simple.

Go for a Squarish Shape

Our current logo fits all the REMUS points. It also works well at different sizes and in multiple locations. You should consider having a logo that can be displayed nicely in small and large sizes, and one that fits nicely in a square. If your logo is tall and skinny or short and wide, it will not work well in some places. Business cards, stationary, packaging, and most websites will all accommodate a logo that easily fits into a square. Long, skinny logos forced into a square space that's part of a web page template, for example, might end up too small to even read. If you decide to sponsor something in the future and your logo will be on a poster next to other company logos, you want it to fit in and compare well.

Countless designers can create logos, and the good ones will automatically deliver REMUS-compliant art. Some designers work at agencies in your local market and others are super-cheap online designers who will do whatever they can to get a logo design commission. When you hire a designer, you shouldn't have to tell them it needs to be big, bold, simple, unique, and memorable. You shouldn't have to tell them it needs to easily fit into a squarish shape. If you have to teach them those requirements, you need to find a different logo artist.

One other word of warning: Once you receive your logo art, you should do a Google image search to see if it matches any other established logo. It is not unheard of for a designer to steal most or all of a good logo design and sell it as their own unique art. This happens more with those cheap, work-for-hire design websites than it does with a local agency, but it's always good to check.

ESTABLISH YOUR DOT-COM

When coming up with your company name, finding an available domain name is actually more important and potentially challenging. And you'll definitely want to get a dot-com domain name. In practically every business, people need to be able to find your business website, and if the name of your business is already taken as a domain name, that can be a challenge.

Your official domain name should be a dot-com, since that was originally established for commercial businesses. If the domain name you'd love to own is taken, you might be tempted to use the exact same domain name and just change the ending to dot-net. Unfortunately, the original dot-net extension was designed to indicate network providers for things like email and hosting services, and the dot-org extension was originally set up to indicate nonprofit organizations. For credibility and clarity of intent, a for-profit business in the United States should use a dot-com domain.

Use Your Imagination for Your Dot-Com Name

In the early days of internet use for commercial businesses in the

United States, getting a domain name that matched your business was less challenging—but even then it wasn't necessarily easy. A newly established home builder in central Florida was building simple, single-family homes in small developments. The company was operating as "Southern Homes" for several years and they wanted the domain name "SouthernHomes.com." Unfortunately, that domain name had been taken by a Texas-based home builder.

At this point, the options were to rename the company based on available domain names or pick a domain name that was simple, memorable, and related to the company. It had to be a dot-com because, based on internet regulations at the time, opting for dot-net or dot-org wasn't even possible. An option like "SouthernHomesInc.com" might have worked, but that was clumsy to say, and in those days consumers might have tried to add a comma or extra period because of the normal way people write "A Company, Inc."

In the end, the solution turned out to be simple, memorable, easy to say and spell, and it even created a feeling of connection between the builder and their clients. Best of all, it was available as a dot-com. They chose "MySouthernHome.com." These days, they wouldn't consider changing their domain name, and "MySouthernHome.com" is painted on the tailgate of their company trucks.

One last note about developing a clever domain name. You may want to avoid including numbers, because people won't know whether to spell out the number or use numerals. Also, avoid anything you can't easily say over the phone—you want to be understood without spelling things out letter by letter. Consider making things simple and memorable up front, so you can save time every single time you say your domain name.

CONSIDER WHETHER TRADEMARKS AND COPYRIGHTS WILL BE IMPORTANT

We aren't attorneys, so what we cover in this book should not be considered legal advice. Always consult with a licensed attorney in good standing for advice about your specific situation.

In certain industries, copyrights and trademarks can be important. If there's a chance someone in your industry might copy the look of your website, logo, or even product design, you might need to get a registered trademark or register your copyright, or patent your design. Each of these considerations has a number of levels and there is always cost involved with registration.

We always include the copyright symbol on our intellectual property (videos, software programs, written materials), followed by the year it was created. We post this within the video itself, on the video credit screens, and also on our website. The statement of copyright has provided legal protections for us when we pursued people or companies who used or resold our materials without permission.

We have a slogan/tagline we use on our website and many of our marketing materials. We registered it as a trademark because we didn't want to take a chance that any other aviation school would use it or something like it. Our slogan is "Courses for Smart, Safe, *FUN* Flying®." This registration is important to us, but it wasn't something we did until we had been in business for years.

THINK ABOUT WEB-FUNDING OPTIONS SUCH AS KICKSTARTER

Some startup-funding websites help inventors and entrepreneurs collect investment money from potential customers before the product is actually available. The concept is to show off your idea with a fancy video and get people to invest in the company in the form of a preorder for something that isn't available yet. That money then funds development without the need for bank loans.

While this might seem good in theory, and it may be easier to secure funding than getting a bank loan or traditional investor, you will need to do careful research. Make sure you comply with all the current procedures required by the platform and follow the appropriate federal or state regulations.

If you want to explore this, you might search "startup-funding website."

INVESTIGATE BUSINESS INCUBATORS

A business incubator is an organization designed to help budding entrepreneurs get their businesses off the ground and profitable at minimal cost. They are usually 501(c)(3) nonprofit organizations, and they come in all shapes and sizes. They may be funded and staffed by other successful, community-minded businesses, economic development councils, chambers of commerce, or a combination of those. They might be as simple as a small office space that hosts occasional seminars for entrepreneurs and provides coaching in various forms. Or they could be as robust as a multi-million-dollar state-of-the-art office complex with shared and private office space at very low prices, with regular meetings, networking, conference and large meeting rooms, and more. Some incubators even offer "maker space" with 3D printing for prototype manufacturing, or commercial kitchens to help startup food processors.

If an incubator might be helpful for meeting space or coaching or any other resources, you should check on availability in your town by asking the chamber of commerce about local incubators and their benefits and costs.

BUYING A BUSINESS COULD BE GOOD (OR GREAT)

Time

You might consider how much time it will save you to buy an existing business that's already in your target market and making a profit. You could save time getting systems in place, gathering inventory, and initial marketing. They've already done a lot of testing, and the results are evident.

Price

If the current owner has personal reasons for wanting to exit their business quickly, it is possible that the price could be better than you would think. This is not something you should necessarily expect, but if this kind of opportunity presents itself, buying an existing business could give you notable advantages.

Customers

Every business needs customers, and if you can buy into a situation where customers are already spending money with a business, you can step into your business with a very realistic projection for income and expenses. Of course, you will want to continue to think of ways to get more customers and think of ways to get current customers to spend more with you. A base of existing customers is incredibly valuable.

Built-In Training and Experience

The current business owner could be a solid source of information about the current market, costs and expenses, good suppliers, competition, and more. If the selling owner is cooperative and willing to share insights and training, this could add even more value to your venture.

BUYING A BUSINESS COULD BE BAD (OR TERRIBLE)

Price

If the current owner assesses the business value by including emotional value or hopeful future projections rather than basing the business value on real-world income and expenses, it is possible that the asking price is too high. The value of a business might diminish shortly after you buy it, for any number of reasons, and these should be included in the value projection. For example, if the current owner has a contract to supply a big customer, and the contract expires in the near future, your business could be hit hard right out of the gate.

Poor Reputation

If the current owner has a bad reputation with customers, suppliers, or the local business community, you will inherit those relationships. Starting from scratch allows you to build a good reputation from a neutral position, but buying a business that has a bad reputation means you will have an even tougher job of reputation building, since it will take work just to get to the same neutral place as a startup.

Location

With many retailers and restaurants, success is often tied closely to location. A location might be in an apparently great part of town, but the lease agreement or restrictions might be bad for your operation.

Equipment Disrepair

If the business you're buying has equipment in need of repair, what looks like an advantage could actually be a disadvantage that needs to be figured into the investment costs. Buying a restaurant with antique cooking equipment, a broken dishwasher, or bad plumbing could keep you from being profitable in alignment with your projections.

JUST REMEMBER — BUYING A BUSINESS IS BUYING THE PAST

Whenever you buy an existing business, you're buying the past of that business and its owner. If it was a well-run, profitable business with good inventory, good customers, and good suppliers at a good price, you could be getting a bargain. But if the current business has a bad history, you'll be buying that, too.

BUSINESSES FOR SALE ARE OFTEN A SECRET

It isn't easy to find all the businesses for sale, because sellers will keep their intent to sell a secret for a host of reasons. In many cases it could be bad for business if employees, suppliers, creditors, the competition, or even customers found out that a business was for sale. So how can you research the availability of a business?

Ask Professionals Who Serve Businesses

People who provide services to businesses are often aware of businesses for sale, and in some cases, they might know when someone *should* sell their business, even if it's not on the market.

Bankers, business lawyers, accountants, and people who work at the Small Business Administration (SBA) are worthwhile sources. Another good resource is the local chamber of commerce. If you are a member, you get a list of all the other members, broken down by category. This can help you collect names of multiple possible businesses you might want to buy.

Call on Businesses Themselves

If you have a business type in mind, like a flower shop or a restaurant, you can call on people who are currently operating those businesses. Ask if they are interested in selling their business or if they know someone who is. You shouldn't worry about how to delicately bring up the subject of whether or not the current business owner wants to sell, just come out and ask. The business owner will take it as a compliment and will almost always perceive that you admire their business.

SETTING THE PRICE AND NEGOTIATING

The main thing that should help you determine the price of a new business is the future profit potential. Tangible assets like inventory and equipment are only important to the extent they contribute to future profits. Once you begin negotiations, you should try to negotiate the price of the business on profits or sales that occur after you buy it. That way, larger portions of your payments are based on the continuing profitability of the business.

VALUATION FOR PROFIT PROJECTIONS

You will want to see the previous owner's tax returns for at least the previous five years to see the reported income.

Consider industry average expenses. The SBA tracks industry average expenses based on the class of business.

Ask the following:

- Is the inventory in salable condition?
- Does the equipment work?
- How reliable/collectible are accounts receivable from existing clients?
- Has the business gained the goodwill of current customers, vendors, or the community?
- Does the business have existing liabilities you'll be assuming with the business purchase?

BUY THE EXISTING BUSINESS WITH LITTLE OR NOTHING DOWN

Using one or more of the following methods for financing could allow you to risk very little while purchasing a business.

Seller Financing

Assuming your research about the profitability is valid and both parties can agree on payments from future profits, seller financing will not only reinforce the assumption that the business is viable, it keeps the risk to a minimum for the new owner and continues to generate income for the current owner with little or no work necessary.

Loans from Suppliers

If the business is a retail operation with products for sale, suppliers may be willing to invest to keep their sales channel open.

Refinancing the Company's Assets

Some businesses have tangible assets that are owned outright by the business, but which have cash value. Refinancing is a possibility, but you could also look into an actual sale where you lease back the equipment.

Effort-Equity

Some business structures allow you to secure financing from a silent partner while investing your own time and effort toward your share or interest in the business. You might consider no salary or a reduced salary for a period of time.

Startup Financing

Following the business incubator concept, some private companies and angel investors have funds available to kick-start new companies. Some of these same funding sources are willing to invest in new owners for existing businesses. Check with your local chamber of commerce and the SBA to see what might be available in your local marketplace.

Escape Clauses

It is always smart to have a licensed attorney review your business purchase agreement to protect your interests. Additionally, you should have one or more escape clauses in case circumstances turn out to be different from what you had been led to believe. These few examples will help you get started:

- <u>Financing</u>
  Purchase is contingent on buyer obtaining satisfactory financing.

- <u>Verification of Inventory</u>
  Purchase is contingent on verification of inventory to buyer's satisfaction.

- <u>Verification of Books</u>
  Purchase is contingent on buyer's inspection of the business accounting records ("the books") and upon buyer's satisfaction with the financial status of the business.

- <u>Accountant's Inspection</u>
  Purchase is contingent on buyer's accountant's inspection of the books and upon buyer's satisfaction with the financial status of the business.

- <u>Attorney's Inspection</u>
  Purchase is contingent on buyer's attorney's inspection of the business and upon buyer's satisfaction with the attorney's report on the status of the business.

GUARD AGAINST RISK

There is no question that legal advice is critical, along with a comprehensive review of the business and inventory, including debts and other commitments. Be sure to investigate any open lines of credit and debts—and that goes beyond simple borrowing. It is possible the business may owe back taxes.

You'll also want to make sure that any assets associated with the business are transferred to your name as the new owner.

Yet another consideration is making sure the exiting business owner does not open a competing business or go to work for a competitor. A well-written noncompete agreement (where allowed by state law) may be worth considering.

GET FREE TRAINING

In most cases, when someone is selling a business they have a strong desire for the new owner to be especially successful. This is both a matter of pride in their former business and a guarantee of future income as structured in the sales agreement. With this in mind, it is very likely that the exiting business owner would be open to helping in the form of training. It would be a good idea to mention this and possibly even include it in the business sales agreement. It is also possible that suppliers would be willing to help you succeed by sharing information and offering training.

DON'T ROCK THE BOAT TOO SOON!

Practically every business owner who buys an existing business has a strong desire to reshape it into something that better reflects their own personality, background, and interests. Resist that urge!

The point is, you bought an existing business with customers and profits *because* it had customers and profits. And making changes before you fully grasp the standard income flow of the business is one of the biggest mistakes people make when buying a business. The standard rule of thumb for something like this is to give yourself at least one year before you make big changes. Changing the menu at a restaurant or changing the sign outside a longtime business might seem like an intelligent "refresh," but these things have made current customers comfortable. You need to reassure customers and vendors that you can keep things going as they were before putting your own stamp on the business.

FRANCHISE

In the early days of our American FleetCare business, we knew we wanted to grow using a franchise structure. Franchise agreements are always structured to favor and protect the parent company, the franchiser, over the franchisee. But we were naïve and unsophisticated and as the franchiser we made some big mistakes. We did not have sufficient leverage over our franchisees to collect the franchise fees they owed us. That's what put us out of business.

There are a couple of takeaways here if you are planning on operating a franchise. First, some franchises may be operated by people who have good intentions but who simply don't have the experience to fully manage their end of the agreement. Additionally, a franchiser who makes the bulk of their money from selling franchises could be a bad business model. The individual franchises need to be reasonably profitable, and you need to do a lot of investigation, if you are considering a franchise that is not a recognized national chain like Subway or McDonald's. Your due diligence should be equivalent to the same research you would do when buying a business.

Whether you are buying a known, recognized franchise or a mostly unknown franchise, you should always talk with current franchisees. Find out about the franchise failure rate. Check out the training for owners, managers, and employees.

Research the Restrictions

Unlike starting your own business or even buying an existing business, buying a franchise is often strictly controlled regarding their offerings, advertising, suppliers, locations, etc. You might not be allowed to operate other businesses or cut costs in ways that make sense to you. Numerous well-known franchises prohibit many kinds of marketing that might help your location. There's even a chicken restaurant franchise that prohibits franchisees from participating in any other business—even if it's not in the food industry. In the end, you might find that owning a franchise is too restrictive for you.

ADVICE FROM A FRANCHISE COACH AND PRO

A good friend has been very successful as a franchisee of Subway and other restaurant chains and retail stores. From his perspective of having owned and sold hundreds of locations, he offers these suggestions:

- Never be the first franchisee.

- Look for a franchiser with at least two hundred franchisees.

- Stay away from the franchise offerings on social media with the slick sizzle-reel videos.

- Look at lots of different franchise opportunities before you decide on one.

- Visit franchise locations and be sure to talk to at least five owners.

- Talk to happy franchise owners as well as disappointed ones, and find out why they hold those views about the franchise. We once visited a failing fast-food location as a customer, and the business was owned and operated by a family who was not from the United States. They had difficulty understanding and being understood by English speakers, and were often unable to understand the order and then prepare the meal customers wanted. When they sold the franchise to an owner who then hired local people who spoke English well, the franchise location quickly became profitable.

- Get a copy of the franchise disclosure document (FDD) for the franchise. You should expect lawsuits listed in the FDD (there always are); see if there are any recurring issues or issues that raise red flags.

- Plan to be personally involved in your first franchise operation before buying additional locations so you can become personally acquainted with all aspects of operating the business.

MORE STRUCTURAL CONSIDERATIONS

You might need to consider other components as you start structuring your business. Consider what kinds of insurance may be necessary for liability coverage in the performance of your business. Is a retail location or office space necessary, or can it be handled from your home? Where will you be banking? What internet hosting and related services will be necessary for sales and communications with clients?

START FLEXING

Once you have tested the viability of your offer, you'll want to start structuring your endeavor as an actual business. As you conservatively start building your business structure (e.g., buying inventory, securing a business license, opening a business bank account, hiring staff), you must remain flexible. That means you should continue to test and be prepared to pivot all the time. You start by exchanging goods or services for money, consistent with your earliest successful testing, but never stop testing. Always be open to new potential markets or adjustments to your offerings that might be more profitable. There is no such thing as a future-proof business. All businesses must change to remain competitive.

As you have learned from earlier chapters, testing comes in many forms. Maybe you adjust your offer based on some A/B market testing. Maybe you survey customers about their experience and implement some of their ideas. But beyond testing, you should also be "SWOT-ing."

SWOT ANALYSIS

Testing takes time and resources, so testing everything you wish you could test isn't always practical. But there's a somewhat less-thorough version of business assessment you can use when you are making decisions: a SWOT analysis.

A SWOT analysis is asking yourself and/or other team members the following questions regarding a business proposal or situation. What are the:

- Strengths
- Weaknesses
- Opportunities
- Threats

Strengths and Weaknesses

Ask yourself, what are the internal strengths and weaknesses of your organization regarding this proposal or situation?

Opportunities and Threats

Ask yourself, what external opportunities and threats does the proposal or situation present to your organization?

Because of the results a SWOT analysis generates, you will benefit by getting in the habit of using it as a thoughtful assessment when you are looking at adding new products or a new line of business. It also helps when looking at competitors and what they offer, or when you are considering proposals and ideas regarding your business.

Let's say your competition comes out with a new product you don't offer. A SWOT analysis will help you and your team determine how you might meet or beat that product. Does their offering do something better than what you currently offer? If so, that would be a threat you need to defend against. Then ask, does their offering represent an opportunity for you? Have they opened up a new market you hadn't considered before? What internal strengths or weaknesses do you have that will help or hinder your response to this external opportunity or threat?

A SWOT analysis isn't just about products or services from competitors—it can be applied to practically anything.

When COVID-19 hit in 2020 and more people wanted to study and work from home, we did a SWOT analysis. We found that our existing strengths of delivering training digitally would open up a marketing opportunity, because more customers would need to study at home, which we enabled. And because we did our business digitally, we were able to accommodate our employees who needed to work from home.

A SWOT analysis is a great way to frame your thinking for anything that shows up in your business, and it will help you think creatively about challenges and opportunities.

LISTEN TO HELPERS (SCORE, SBA, CHAMBER, INDUSTRY SITES, AND MAGAZINES)

One of the great things about being a new entrepreneur is that a lot of people want you to succeed. Other successful businesspeople are frequently willing to provide advice and insights to help you on your journey. In many cases, the advice is free.

SCORE

The U.S. Small Business Association is an even larger organization, with resources and training designed to help small businesses. You can find guides for researching, launching, managing, and growing your business, and many of their guides are complimentary to what we teach entrepreneurs. They have funding programs, access to local resources, and online training for entrepreneurs. When we bought our office and video studio building for King Schools, a significant part of the funds came from an SBA-insured loan. Have a look at their offerings online at sba.gov.

Industry Sites, Magazines, and Trade Shows

In almost every field, you'll find clubs and trade groups, websites, newsletters, blogs, vlogs, and in many cases, YouTube channels related to your industry. Have a look at these resources to stay on top of what's happening in your industry so you can apply a SWOT analysis to anything new or interesting. Your business can benefit from understanding and analyzing emerging trends. It always pays to keep current in your field.

SOME WAYS TO PROTECT YOURSELF

As we briefly covered already, it may be possible to protect your business, an invention, a logo, or your written or recorded materials by using patents, trademarks, or copyrights. None of these protections should be considered a "lock," though. In other words, it's possible a patent might protect your business from competitors who make an exact duplicate of something you invented and that you manufacture and sell. However, it is also possible that your competition could legally create something similar, but with just a few differences, and that might take sales from your customer base.

If you're considering any of these protection methods, you can plan on spending money on legal services and on having protections for a limited time and in limited ways. You'll need to evaluate the costs compared to the apparent protections.

Other protections might involve requiring employees to sign a noncompete agreement so they don't leave your business to go to work for a competitor. The scope of these agreements is limited and varies from state to state, so it's worth your while to check with legal counsel or an HR firm.

Do what you can to protect yourself with legal documents and signed agreements, but don't rely on these protections to always work 100 percent, as you wish they would. Also, if you have trade secrets that help your business be profitable, keep those secrets from all your employees who don't absolutely need to know them.

KEEP TESTING AND PRUNING (AND FOLLOW THE 80/20 RULE)

As you get your business off the ground, keep testing. Keep pivoting. Do a regular SWOT analysis. And every once in a while, look at your sales and expenses and apply the 80/20 rule.

Once you have a growing inventory or service offering, you might find that one particular offering only generates a little income, but it requires a large amount of your resources. Ask yourself if removing that item from the mix would help you be more profitable and free up resources to invest in the aspects of your business that are especially profitable.

At King Schools, in the days when we used to ship videos (VHS, CDs, and DVDs) to our customers, we decided to leverage our existing shipping department and customer lists. We sold products that did not compete with our courses but that were of interest to the same people who would buy aviation training. For example, we could buy GPS navigation units wholesale and sell them to our customers. Over time, we moved to fully digital delivery of our courses, so eventually the only items we were shipping were third-party products. We applied the 80/20 rule and determined that 80 percent of our management time and business expenses were related to selling and shipping other people's products, and that generated only 20 percent of our income. We eliminated that part of the business, which allowed us to restructure our business and invest more money and staff resources into the creation of even more all-digital courses, resulting in an even better profit margin.

SUMMARY

Obviously, there are many tools and techniques for structuring and running a new business. This chapter has addressed many useful tools as we've shared our experience and the experiences of other successful entrepreneurs. We have used many of these tools and skipped the ones that didn't apply to our business model. Use what you need in your business, based on your personal skill set and what your business will offer, and always remember to keep testing, adjusting, and "SWOT-ing."

GOAL SETTING IN OUR LIVES

I vividly remember that Martha and I had set aside some time to talk with each other about the future, in the bedroom we had set up as an office. We had put our courses on video and we were just beginning to sell the video courses by direct mail. This represented a new business for us and we wanted to take time to talk about what our expectations would be. We talked about the change in our personal lives from the transition—from spending our lives traveling to teach seminars to spending our time in a studio recording our courses. It was a big change for us.

I remember that when I suggested to Martha how much money I hoped we might be able to make in the new business, her eyes misted over. I said, "What's wrong?" She said, "I am not sure I can guarantee you that." I assured her that I would be happy with our partnership even if we fell short of that goal.

Today we are making thirty times the goal I suggested. My take-away from that experience is that it is not so important what the goal you set is. What is important is that you *have* a goal. If we had not set some kind of goal, I am certain we would not be doing as well as we are now.

John

7

USING SIMPLE, CREATIVE BUSINESS CONTROLS

As an entrepreneur, you are following your passions. It's easy to get caught up in one or more of your favorite passions and pay little or no attention to minding the store (which many of us find a lot less fun).

CASH, NOT INCOME, PAYS YOUR BILLS

It's fairly common for entrepreneurs to generate income statements that provide an overview of their business's profitability, and as long as the revenue numbers are bigger than the expense numbers, they're happy. That report feels good. Unfortunately, a positive income statement with the promise of future income alone won't pay the bills. It won't feed you. Profit alone won't pay employees. You need cash in the bank to make those things happen.

CASH CAN STILL RUN SHORT WITH STRONG INCOME STATEMENTS

If you're selling products, it takes cash to replace inventory. If you have employees, you need cash to pay them regularly. An income statement that indicates a large profit can give you a false sense of security, because even in a service business it's possible to appear as if you are in a good financial position when you're at risk of running out of cash. This is especially true of a growing business, because inventory and materials have to be bought and employees have to be paid in advance at an even greater rate when the business is growing.

For example, let's say you're in the business of cabinet installation and you get a new client who is a builder and is projecting a half-dozen installations per week for a few months. Even if you're not responsible for the cost of the cabinets, you may need to hire more installers, and that costs money. All your workers will expect a weekly check, and if your agreement is to receive payment for completed work each month, cash could be a problem. It's common for cabinet deliveries to be wrong. Incorrect hardware, wrong-size cabinets, or homes that aren't ready for the installation (because another subcontractor didn't finish the drywall, for example) can throw you off schedule. And if your customer, the contractor, doesn't like the way the trim is installed or some other small cosmetic issue, they could refuse to pay you until it's changed.

CASH FLOW STATEMENTS ARE THE WAY TO GO — STAY CURRENT

A cash flow statement projects your expected cash receipts and expenditures for a period of time, helping you anticipate cash income and outflow mismatches for that period of time.

How Often?

Popular wisdom suggests that your cash reports should be generated at a rate that is reasonable for your type and size of business. That may be weekly, monthly, or quarterly, but we recommend that you develop a way to leverage your accounting system to create cash flow reports weekly. You may not always need to review them weekly, but the reports should be available.

King Schools is a multi-million-dollar business that's forty-five years old, and we get a bank balance report for each of our bank accounts every single day. We get a weekly cash flow report so we know what's coming in and going out each week. And by paying attention to the daily bank balances most days, and our weekly cash flow reports, we can quickly spot trends and see upcoming events that might be problematic.

If you get in the habit of following your balances like this from the start, it will only take a few minutes total each week to review your finances. That way you'll avoid unpleasant surprises.

Of course, we also get monthly income statements. We require our accounting department to have the statements available by the tenth of the following month. That way we have current information about our profitability and can make informed decisions about any changes we might need. Income statements that are three or four months old when you receive them are pretty much worthless for decision-making.

Continuous Reports Make You Smart, Popular with Vendors, and More Successful

It isn't enough to generate cash balance reports, cash flow statements, and income statements. You need to use them in all your business decision-making processes, especially as you grow from startup to a medium-sized business. Cash is your performance indicator, and a sufficient cash balance is the needed green light for purchases of equipment, hiring staff, paying for vendor services, and other costs associated with growth.

Too many entrepreneurs find out the hard way that purchase or investment decisions that are based on hope don't usually work out the right way. Income statements based on payments that are not yet collected are a form of hope. Granted, they are based on the promise that customers will pay what they owe, but there are always times when those payments are delayed or don't happen at all. Making purchase decisions based on hope is always a gamble.

When you start making purchase decisions based on the actual cash you have in the bank, you'll naturally slow your purchase decisions and expansion plans and build in margins for contingencies. It can feel like you're moving too slow, but there are rewards. You're far less likely to be caught off guard when a customer who has always paid on time suddenly misses a payment or pays slowly for some reason. You will be appreciated by your vendors when you are a customer who always pays on time. You will make better purchasing decisions when they are based on good pricing and service, not on who can give you financing for the purchase. In the end, you will be more successful when you don't have to waste time frantically, inefficiently chasing cash.

As you consider a purchase, it is wise to first look at your cash flow statements for an understanding of actual cash on hand, not your projected income statements. Then ask yourself, "Do I have enough cash to pay for this while still easily managing my regular operating expenses?" As soon as you can, you should also have cash reserves in case a situation arises that unexpectedly slows your regular income flow for a month or two.

Slight Disappointments and Business Wins

Over the years, we have developed a love of accumulating cash. While some people enjoy spending money, we have a distaste for spending cash. However, as we have applied this approach to investments and purchases, we've sometimes experienced negative results—mostly in the belief that we might be missing out on profits that could come from spending sooner. Reluctance to spend cash on new equipment caused us to be slow in moving from VHS to CDs and then to DVDs. Because we have the habit of accumulating cash, not only did we need to make sure we had enough cash on hand to purchase the new duplicating machines, we also had to be sure that the likelihood of a payoff was more certain than just a guess or feeling. We wanted to make sure we weren't moving to a new technology that promised to be the future but turned out to be a flash-in-the-pan technology that wasn't sufficiently adopted by the masses. Remember LaserDiscs or Betamax video players?

In retrospect, we were slow to move to newer video delivery options. We were slow to buy our office building and build the video studio in it. We were slow to hire. But we were always able to maintain profitability, and we have lots of cash in the bank and lots of options because of it.

Have Cash Available for Payments with Regular Vendors

In the days when we paid a small print shop to print the mailers for our ground-school classes, we would frequently pay cash up front when we placed the order, instead of when we picked it up or after receiving a bill. The print shop especially appreciated it when, after they had a fire, we took them cash in advance for the next six months of our printing. That kept them in business when otherwise they would have had to shut down.

From then on, no matter how busy the print shop was at the time, our jobs automatically got priority and our mailers were always on time.

Cash Reserves Matter Too

Maintaining cash reserves makes it easier to cope with the unexpected curveballs that occur in every business. Over time, having cash reserves just makes life easier in every respect.

BEFORE EXTENDING CREDIT

In all different kinds of businesses—for instance, if you're installing fencing, taking professional portraits, or even delivering software or digital training—you can find yourself being asked to extend credit to customers. The good news is that there are so many ways to accept digital payments today, and so many credit cards are available, that most businesses no longer need to take on the role of financing purchases.

Services like PayPal, Stripe, Square, and many others allow companies to accept digital payments or credit card payments with very little trouble. In the past, you had to buy special credit card terminal machines and connect them through your bank, but it's all much easier now. Modern digital payment systems can generate a digital invoice that can be emailed, paid, and confirmed before products are delivered to the customer. These transactions can happen instantaneously, just like at a grocery store cash register. You can take credit card payments in person with a ten-dollar Square card reader attached to your smartphone. You can buy these at any electronics store or at Target.

Note: Our mention of these services is not an endorsement. Do your research and work with your bank to see what the most trouble-free, reliable electronic payment system(s) would work best with your business structure and your bank. Some of these newer online payment organizations have terms that allow them to withhold large amounts of money, even if goods or services have been delivered. Digital payment clearing through the bank where you have your business account is much less likely to incur these types of financial roadblocks, though if you do experience a bank payment hold, they could also freeze your business checking account. It's best to spread your risk across multiple money-processing services.

At King Schools, we rarely extend credit to our clients. We have structured our business in such a way that clients do not ask us to provide this kind of additional service. Nevertheless, we recognize that some businesses will not be able to demand prepayment because of how their industry works. For example, if you want to sell a food product at a major grocery-store chain or big box store, you will almost always be asked to provide inventory first, and you will only be paid when it sells. A big chain can get away with this because they have the leverage of their store locations and visibility.

Before you actually decide to extend credit, even to a highly reputable national store chain, ask yourself, "If I lost everything my customer owes me, how bad off would I be?" Until you can confirm that losing all the money owed to you would not put you out of business, you should look for other customers or other ways to sell your products or services.

DON'T EXTEND CREDIT OR EVEN JUST DO BUSINESS WITH ONLY ONE BIG CLIENT

You've heard the old adage "Don't put all your eggs in one basket." That phrase is considered common knowledge because it has proven to be great advice time and again in so many arenas.

If you come up with a hot new product or service that some big company wants to buy, it's easy to get lulled into a sense of security that you'll be doing business with this big player with big budgets and they're sure to pay. After all, they have plenty of money—don't they? Don't count on it!

A good friend of ours was doing business with a Fortune 100 company and had a great working relationship with them. Because of their agreement, he was frequently netting $6K per month from them back in the early 2000s. As their orders increased, he needed to fund their delivery. Since the company had paid on time every month for more than a year, our friend began extending credit for their orders using an American Express Gold Card to pay for his up-front expenses. Then one month, a receipt he submitted to the company for reimbursement (under $20) was hard to read, so the company put his entire $30K invoice for services rendered and expenses on hold. This caused him to miss his Amex payment and his card was blocked for additional spending. Our friend had to scramble and borrow cash from relatives to make ends meet for two weeks.

In the end, everything worked out and he paid back American Express and his relatives, but his credit had a blemish and he started operating his business differently. After that stressful predicament, his working relationship with this once-loved client was a bit less comfortable.

COLLECTIONS COMPANIES

If you decide to provide a line of credit for a client and they don't pay on time, work through the process of attempting to collect funds in a way that is consistent with practices in your industry. Follow the advice of your accountant regarding what kinds of late notices you should send and the terms stated on those notices. If the late-paying client is a personal friend, a friendly phone call would probably be a good first step.

As the outstanding invoice continues to age, follow your accountant or banker's advice regarding next steps. At some point you may need to turn the account over to a collections agency if the balance merits the trouble and expense.

INVENTORY AND ACCOUNTING REPORTS — SEPARATE THE DUTIES

In many businesses, in addition to your accounting reports you'll also have inventory reports so you can manage those assets appropriately. With both reports, as well as your systems for managing accounting and inventory, things are different when employees are involved. When you get to the point where you hire staff to handle various operations, it is always a good practice to divide the responsibility between certain activities such as managing inventory and bank balances.

Our accountant prepares checks but does not have the authority to sign them. We have always managed our bank accounts this way. Similarly, we have learned to keep inventory responsibilities divided so that no one person can physically take something out of inventory and also change the computerized inventory report to hide that the item was removed.

But even with this plan, we've had the occasional oversight that resulted in an occurrence of employee theft. A few years ago, we had an employee who worked in the shipping department and was responsible for receiving packages of returned items from customers, like GPS units, and putting the returned units back on the shelf. The employee would then pass the paperwork on to an employee in the accounting department, who would electronically add the item back into the computerized inventory records. No one person had access to take something out of inventory and then hide the theft by adjusting the inventory count. We thought we were covered.

The bug in the system happened when the shipping department employee's manager thought it would be OK to teach the employee to not only put returned items back on the shelf, but to also electronically add those items back into inventory. The idea was that the customer would receive their refund more quickly.

The employee soon realized that since he could *increase* the inventory count when a GPS was returned to inventory from a customer, he could also *reduce* the inventory count and then take a GPS from inventory and sell it to a local pawnshop. The electronic inventory count would still match the physical units on the shelf.

It turned out this employee had a gambling problem and was in desperate need of money, and these GPSs were worth about a thousand dollars each. Once he had gotten away with a single GPS unit theft, he started doing it on a regular basis.

Because the inventory numbers reflected what was on the shelf, we only discovered a problem when our profit margins for GPS sales were surprisingly low. That triggered a manual inventory reconciliation process that caught the problem. But it could have been caught much earlier, or stopped before it started, if the thief hadn't had such complete access to both the units themselves and our computerized inventory system. It was no favor to the employee and proved to be an insurmountable temptation to him.

INVENTORY REPORTS

As you can see, inventory management of hard goods is an important part of your business if you sell physical products. This means you need to have a system to enter newly received inventory and check it out when it gets sold.

Use good judgment when determining how often to run inventory reconciliation reports and how precisely to manage inventory. If you have thousands and thousands of five-cent trinkets, it is definitely not a worthwhile practice to count them all on a regular basis. On the other hand, if you are running a small jewelry store, it is probably a very good idea to have a system that tracks inventory precisely and very frequently. The rule of thumb is to not waste time keeping track of items when it costs you more to keep track of them than they actually cost. Office supplies like pencils and stationery fall into that category.

INDICATORS OF BUSINESS HEALTH

Understanding Your Sales Reports

In addition to checking your income statements and cash reports, you need to regularly understand how your sales are going. How many units did you sell today or this week or this month? What was the source of your sales? How many sales from which internet ads or direct mail flyers or salesperson? Which items are selling better? Then compare week to week and see if there are any trends.

Using Your Income Statement

Despite the fact that you should use cash analysis as a more accurate decision-making tool and indicator of your business health from day to day, the role of your income statement is to provide an analysis tool for looking at the bigger picture and trends over a longer period of time. What months of the year were best for sales? Were there any industry trends that drove business? Did the introduction of a new product or service boost business? What items are losing profitability? What products or services merit being cut from the business? Are the profit margins of various lines what they should be? If the answer is no, could it be a sign that inventory is being stolen?

Learning from the Balance Sheet

Your balance sheet lists your assets and liabilities as of a certain date. Just as with your income statement, information is most relevant if it shows several different periods and compares them to one another. Compare figures to the same time period from the previous year and pay closer attention to the percentages than the dollars.

Can You Pay the Bills?

One balance sheet ratio that really helps you keep a close eye on the financial health of your business is the current ratio. That is the ratio of current assets to current liabilities.

- Current assets are those that can be converted into cash within a year.
- Current liabilities are those that will be paid in less than a year.

This ratio shows how much you have in assets that could quickly be converted into cash, relative to the short-term bills you owe.

To find the current ratio, divide the total amount of current assets by the total amount of current liabilities. Current assets include cash, inventory, and accounts receivable, but not any expenses you have pre-paid, because you usually can't get your money back from them. Current liabilities include accounts payable to your suppliers and others, and loan payments due within the year.

It is usually considered good policy for a store or a manufacturing operation to maintain a current ratio of about 2:1. This means you have twice as much money in assets (that can be converted relatively quickly to cash) as what you owe in current bills. If your current ratio starts dropping significantly over time, and particularly if it is below that two-to-one standard, that indicates possible future trouble in paying your bills when they come due.

Determining Inventory Turnover

As we covered earlier, inventory reports are important to make sure valuable items aren't being taken from you, but there's another way you should use inventory reports as a gauge of your business health. How frequently does inventory turn over?

In the 1980s and '90s, when we taught this aspect of entrepreneurship, we had a formula for calculating approximate annual inventory turnover. These days there are inventory management systems that can do this much more accurately, and those systems can even be structured to trigger notifications when inventory numbers are getting low (to trigger a reorder) or piling up (to trigger smaller future orders).

The key is to use these systems to manage inventory so you aren't overstocked and so you don't run short for projected future demand.

CONTRIBUTION MARGIN/BREAK-EVEN ANALYSIS IS A GREAT "WHAT IF" ANALYSIS TOOL

We use the visualization tool we are about to describe to evaluate everything from a single, small, salable product or service up to and including entire branches of a business. It can be used to evaluate proposed items (products, services, or branches of business) or existing items to determine what to keep and what to eliminate, where to invest more and where to pull back.

The first part of the tool is the calculation of what we call the "contribution margin analysis." (A sample worksheet is at the end of this chapter.) It is the margin (or profit) left after deducting all direct variable expenses when a product or service is sold.

Start with the gross income the item (product or service) generates and deduct all the variable costs associated with creating and delivering the item. To use this tool properly, you should only apply variable costs to the contribution margin analysis and avoid allocating any fixed costs. Variable costs are incurred specifically because of that product or service. Fixed costs are expenses you have which aren't specifically incurred in creating that product or service.

Think of it this way: If the item goes away, all the variable costs associated with its creation, marketing, selling, and delivery should also go away. Fixed costs, like the cost of your office space and (usually) staff, do not go away with the discontinuation of any particular product or service.

The "what if" aspect of the contribution margin analysis allows you to brainstorm by changing one or more variables (such as a change in sales price, a change in production cost, or a change in the sales commission). You will also need to make an educated guess about what that change might do to your total sales of that item, and whether that would improve or harm your profitability. The analysis can also help you determine how much you would need to raise the price or cut some cost to keep an item profitable if some cost outside your control goes up. Once you map out the hypothetical adjustments, you can start testing your adjusted product or service offerings to see if your estimates are correct.

The second part of the tool is the calculation of what we call the "break-even analysis." The purpose of segregating fixed and variable costs is that it lets you figure out how many units of a product you have to sell in a specified period of time in order to cover a certain amount of the fixed costs of your business in that same time period.

Let's say you want to cover $1,000 of fixed costs per month with the sales of a certain product, and that product gives you $10 of contribution margin for each unit you sell. If you divide the $1,000 of fixed costs by $10, you will see that you would need to sell a hundred units in order to cover that $1,000 of fixed costs.

So if your fixed expenses were $1,000, your break-even point would be the sales of one hundred units.

Years ago, we created a simple worksheet as a starting point to help us lay out all the variable expenses tied to an item, so we could change one or more variables and see how this might affect our bottom line. Use this contribution margin/break-even analysis worksheet as a starting point for developing your own "what if" analysis, and add or change variables to fit your specific business. Excel spreadsheets are really great for making it easy to change the variables when you're evaluating those "what if" scenarios.

Sample Contribution Margin/Break-Even Analysis Worksheet
Contribution Margin Analysis

Product/service/line of business to analyze:

_____   Date: _____

Net sales per unit sold: $_____

<u>Variable expenses per unit sold</u>

Production expenses:

       Direct product cost $_____

       Direct labor $_____

Total production expenses $_____

Marketing/sales expenses:

      Advertising:

           Direct mail $_____

           Web ads $_____

           SEO $_____

           Print ads $_____

           Other $_____

Sales commissions $_____

Credit expenses $_____

Total marketing/sales expenses $_____

Total direct expenses $_____

Estimated *variable* overhead expenses $_____

(Expenses that would go away if you quit selling the product/service)

Total variable expenses $_____

Contribution margin per unit sold $_____

Break-Even Analysis

Estimated fixed overhead expenses per timeframe (week, month, year)
being evaluated $_____

Break-even number of units per timeframe (week, month, year)

_____

(To find the break-even number of units, divide the fixed overhead by
the contribution margin per unit.)

CHAPTER

8

MULTIPLYING YOUR EFFORTS THROUGH SMART HIRING

Your passions may empower you, but you may decide you can't do it alone.

You may, in most cases, decide that as an entrepreneur you want to multiply your efforts by soliciting team members to fulfill customer needs and wants. The primary reason most entrepreneurs decide to hire employees is to gain the benefit of their knowledge and skills.

As entrepreneurs, we have brought our own passions and knowledge to our business. What prompted us years ago to bring employees into the business was the need for expertise we didn't have. Today, our contribution is primarily establishing and reinforcing the core values of the business.

One of the core values we want everyone in our business to embrace and practice is our approach to communication. Our philosophy is that all communications with someone should be focused on them, not us. Our policy is that all letters, texts, or emails from King Schools should begin with the words "you" or "your." After all, why would we be communicating with others if the message wasn't about them?

Similarly, we insist that our ads be focused on customers, not the company. We have found that focusing on the customer is very effective and gets great results. Focusing on others is our strongest core value.

When we hire new employees, we look them in the eyes and explain, "It is our obligation to provide you with meaningful and rewarding work in an atmosphere of civility and respect. If you feel that is not what you are experiencing, we want you to come and tell us so in person."

When we are talking about "meaningful and rewarding work," we are recognizing that work needs to be meaningful to employees and rewarding for them. When we talk about an atmosphere of civility and respect, we mean that our employees must receive civility and respect from everyone—us, fellow employees, customers, and vendors. If we see it isn't happening, we will take steps to ensure it does.

An employee devotes their most precious resource, their time, to our company. We respect and appreciate that and seek to ensure their time is appreciated. The employees provide much of the expertise of our business, and we respect them for that. One of our greatest privileges in life is to be associated with the competent people who work with us.

WHEN HIRING MAKES SENSE

You will decide to hire employees when you feel that you will benefit from doing so—primarily by making more money. The decision certainly complicates your business.

Your hiring needs to be strategic—it needs to happen at the right time. It is very common for entrepreneurs to get in a rush to hire because they erroneously believe they don't have a business until they have employees. As you recall, you don't have a business until you have identified a customer need or want you can fulfill profitably. Hiring needs to result in an overall increase in profitability. Hiring should be done only after you have evaluated the costs and payoffs associated with filling a particular position.

WHEN HIRING DOESN'T MAKE SENSE

You need to ask yourself a handful of questions before you pull the trigger and hire an employee. One of the questions should *not* be—even subconsciously—"Will hiring someone make my business appear more successful?" or "Will hiring someone help me avoid the parts of the business I don't like?"

The biggest single expense on the income statement of most small businesses is employees. Every dollar you pay to an employee is a dollar that does not go into your pocket or into cash reserves to apply toward future business growth. Managing expenses, and specifically hiring expenses, is the largest single determinant to the profitability of your business.

Every entrepreneur should delay hiring until it becomes clear that *not* hiring is costing you money. It is usually beneficial to have a bias against hiring. Delaying hiring is much more than just delaying the direct costs of the employee such as pay and benefits. It also delays ancillary expenses related to hiring, including training and supervising. And while we don't like to think of these things, there is the possibility of theft and the related expenses of creating systems that minimize that risk.

WHEN NOT HIRING STARTS TO COST YOU MONEY

For most small businesses, it only makes sense to hire employees when the lack of labor has clearly become the biggest single obstacle to increased profit. Notice the issue is increased *profit*, not increased growth or even increased productivity. When you hire employees, very often you'll find that you've only increased your management burden and increased the number of dollars going through the business, without keeping any more dollars for yourself. You will want to make sure that the addition of employees will result in more dollars in your pocket or in cash reserves before you make the decision to hire.

HIDDEN EMPLOYEE COSTS

Employees are the biggest expense for most businesses, but in some cases employee expenses are unnecessarily high. That happens when there's high turnover. Not only do you have the hard cost of paying employees, you also have the costs associated with the hiring process and training. High turnover can cause you to incur these additional costs without the associated increased employee output.

AVOID UNNECESSARY EMPLOYEE EXPENSES BY GETTING A BIT MORE FORMAL

If you start out on your own and you have help in the earliest stages of your business from family and very close friends, you'll need to add an additional resource before hiring your first non-family member. You need a written plan for the business that describes goals, workflows, job responsibilities, and customer interactions. This isn't the same thing as a business plan with big-picture goals and financial targets. This is more akin to an employee manual with job goals and company policies.

When it's just you and family members (and possibly a close friend or two), you can get by with many aspects of the business "in your head." When you have employees, that just doesn't work as well. You will benefit from a written reference that will answer questions about your business philosophy and policies when you're not available. And don't forget that you'll need to include policies in writing for handling inventory and cash as part of the training.

An additional consideration of your written plan is that *you* need to be tuned into the plan and follow it as well. Shortcuts that used to be OK when it was just you will be disruptive. When you follow the written procedures, you set an example for employees and you prevent confusion about what you're doing or how something got done.

THE SECRET TO GETTING THE BEST WORKERS

In the same way that you need to sell to customers, you need to sell to potential employees. For customers, you need to deliver something for which they are willing to trade their hard-earned money—they should feel like they have acquired something more valuable than their money. When you sell an employee on working for your company, you must meet their needs for income, benefits, and accomplishment. Also, they should understand that they play an important part in the process of delivering something of value to customers and improving the lives of others along the way. When you sell to a customer, you are asking them to trade their money for what you're selling. When you sell to an employee, you are asking them to devote their time and skills to a beneficial outcome for the company in exchange for money, benefits, and meaningful and rewarding work.

UNDERSTANDING HIRING BASICS

When it comes to hiring people to perform certain aspects of work with a company, you need to consider the necessary skill level for that position. In your specific business, you might need someone with a particular certification or professional expertise, or you might need manual labor to do repetitive tasks that can be taught to numerous people, or you might need a mix of moderately skilled to highly skilled people.

Interestingly, we once had a very kind-hearted manager in our shipping and duplication department who had a passion for helping people who had fallen on hard times in their lives. These people often had challenges that had caused them to be in treatment, and then released to a halfway house so they could acclimate to society. Our manager would work with local halfway houses to help people looking for a job. We hired many of them when shipping and duplication were important parts of our business, and our manager did a great job with those employees. This wasn't always a smooth process, because some of these participants occasionally broke halfway house rules by not spending the night there, and we hosted several visits from local police who would meet and talk with the rule breakers. But thanks to the commitment of our dedicated manager, a lot of people received wonderful opportunities and we never had any big problems.

WE HIRE KNOWLEDGE

The interview and hiring process can be a little more challenging with positions that require higher skill levels. At King Schools, we think of this as hiring "knowledge." In some cases, we have hired professionals who have skill sets that overlap with ours, such as our CEO. But we also hire people who have skills needed for our video training business who are well beyond our skill level. We have hired video recording and editing experts, audio experts, and software experts. Sometimes we started out by using companies that provided those services. Once we determined it would be more cost effective and profitable to have those services fully in-house, we created an internal position and hired for that role.

TO FIND THEM, GO WHERE SKILLED PEOPLE ARE LIKELY TO BE

Even in the age of the internet, you can still find in-person meetings, clubs, and associations you can visit and join to find skilled professionals. To start your search, look for those kinds of groups so you can join or attend as a guest. The great thing about this approach is that you get to meet prospects in person before they even know they are prospects. Plus, you are meeting people whose passion for that field of interest is so strong they have taken the time to join a club or association.

For example, if your business will need a full-time photographer or videographer, you can search for photography clubs or independent filmmaking clubs in your area. You can attend meetings and try to make connections. Besides the fact that these people are obviously passionate enough about their field to join a club, they aren't usually in "selling mode" at these meetings because they're surrounded by other photographers or filmmakers. They are not defensive and you can simply engage with people discussing their passion.

With our direct-marketing passion, it was only natural for us to join the San Diego Direct Marketing Club. We went to meetings to learn and share, and when it came time to hire a direct-marketing professional, we already had an idea of who we would approach.

Of course, today you can do similar things online. There are professional groups on Facebook, and LinkedIn has options for finding people with the skills you're interested in. However, you might have to do a bit more research after you find a candidate online, because it is harder to get to know a person well online than it is in person, where you can casually talk about their passions.

Another thing you can do, depending on the type of website your company has, is to post job openings on your site. This works well for us because we teach pilots, and many pilots who visit our site have valuable skills in addition to their love of flying. Many would simply love to work at King Schools. We have found a number of great employees using this method. If your site is frequented by a lot of visitors, that method may be worth considering.

CONDUCTING THE INTERVIEW

By the time you start conducting interviews to fill a position, you will need a complete job description and a written set of employee guidelines. Your overall goal will be to see how well each candidate matches the skill set necessary for that position. But there are a handful of things you will want to look for to help assess which candidate would be best for the position. And you should remember that the interview is also a form of selling. You will want to include elements that help you sell the benefits of working for your company to prospective employees.

Whenever we have a job candidate come to our offices at King Schools, we make sure to show them the photo gallery in our main entrance hallway. This is where we have a photograph of every single employee with their name and title, grouped with the other people in that department. This gives us a great opportunity to visually explain to a potential employee the structure of King Schools and what the different departments do. Plus, all our employees can quickly see who the person was that passed them in the hallway or parked near them earlier that day. New employees especially appreciate this resource. If you don't have a building yet but you have several employees, you can easily manage an online photo display. Just be sure to keep it someplace where employees can access it easily.

Beyond looking for the necessary job skills, we are always looking for employees for whom it is in their makeup to seek out and fulfill the needs of customers, fellow employees, and vendors. We are looking for people who have the right habit of helping others. Over the years, we have found that interviewees who mainly talk about themselves are usually not sufficiently oriented toward helping others. But when we find candidates who excitedly talk about our business, that piques our interest. Some of the best candidates are the ones who not only express what excites them about our business but also how they will fit in and complement the company's mission.

There is definitely a level of maturity involved when an entrepreneur looks at a job interview as a selling opportunity in order to make the available position as attractive and exciting as possible to the right candidate. This was a weakness in our first businesses, but we like to think we have gotten much better about considering the needs of our job candidates. We try to always emphasize our company's unique selling proposition (USP), our company's mission to help customers, and our company values. We are not only proud of these elements of our business philosophy, but we also want to make sure all our employees share similar enthusiasm for these important aspects of our business.

TESTING

Properly completing a job application, submitting a cover letter, and providing a quality CV or résumé are all expected for many professional positions. Beyond that, however, there are times when you might consider testing prospective employees for a skill set that needs to be used on the job. You don't always have to rely on just an interview, a résumé, and a couple of positive recommendations. You can ask how the job candidate would handle a particular situation.

At King Schools, we have software department candidates do a coding exercise. In our course production department, we have job candidates write brief descriptions about how they would teach a subject. This kind of testing gives us valuable insight about each candidate's skill set. If your business would benefit from this kind of insight, consider providing time for it during your interview process.

This kind of exercise also tests the ability of the prospect to communicate well, which is a skill that will be valuable for their entire association with your company.

EMPLOYEE TRAINING

You already know that before you even interview your first job candidate, you should have created a comprehensive job description and set of company guidelines—these will help employees navigate their job and understand company policies. Providing these and reinforcing them with your new employees will be critical during training. We have always done this to one degree or another, even with our earliest businesses.

In the early days of our business, however, we overlooked the *most* important things you should include in employee training: our company mission to help others, our Unique Selling Proposition (USP), and our core values regarding employees. Now we're sure to include these things during the interview process, during training, and repeatedly as a part of our everyday interactions at the office. In fact, our company mission statement and our USP are posted on the wall beside our employee pictures, and our commitment to our employees, the essence of our core values, are on our website in the "About King Schools" section.

Our mission: Seek out and take care of the needs of customers, coworkers, and vendors.

Our USP: Take relatively complicated material, clarify it, simplify it, and make it fun.

Our core values: Provide meaningful and rewarding work in an atmosphere of civility and respect.

You'll want to make a commitment right now to develop your own company mission, USP, and commitment to employees. You should also commit to using these items in your interview process and training, and make sure these items continue to be a part of your daily corporate culture. Your employees might go so far as to share the company mission and USP with customers, as our employees often do. Continuously looking at interactions between customers, prospective customers, fellow employees, vendors, and management will help maintain a positive corporate culture with committed employees, customers, and vendors.

We hope our examples help inspire and inform your own company's mission, unique selling proposition, and core values. You're welcome to adopt them if you feel like they fit your style. They have served us quite well over the years.

A USP PAYOFF EXAMPLE

To give you an idea of the role our USP plays in our course creation at King Schools, here's an example: it is a regular occurrence that one of our employees restates our USP before we begin filming a course. Then, at any given point during the presentation and taping of the course materials, if one of our team members suggests that a particular element of a script actually complicates a concept rather than simplifying it, we meet as a group, right there on the spot, and determine if there is a better way to convey the course content. Our USP opens the door for employees to be involved in a collaborative effort. It yields a much better finished product because they have been directly invited to refine our efforts in order to deliver a course that takes relatively complicated material, clarifies it, simplifies it, and makes it fun.

TRAINING ELEMENTS FOR YOUR BUSINESS

When you consider that we are in the business of teaching people via video, it is only natural that we have quite a few internal-use videos to teach our employees how to do things at King Schools. Practically any business with more than just a couple of employees could create simple videos using the amazing camera on a smartphone. However, just because it is convenient and easy doesn't mean you can be sloppy about the training videos for your employees. You don't have to worry about high-end video production, but you do need to include clear, concise instructional information about various processes, procedures, and job functions within your company.

Screen-capture video programs for Mac and PC can also be used to show people processes and procedures on computer screens. A common practice for many modern businesses is to record computer processes, website access, internal software data entry systems, etc., and save the training videos to a shared drive so employees anywhere in the world can access them. To create a usable training video, you'll want to use a good microphone and capture a narrated explanation as part of the screen-capture video training.

PAYING EMPLOYEES

Profit, of course, is a legitimate motivation for both the company and its employees.

The employees need to be paid a fair amount based on the quality of job the employee is capable of doing, the responsibilities assigned to them, and the local marketplace. Paying a weak employee more money does not make them any better—it simply costs more. If you have a poorly performing employee, you cannot improve their motivation and/or competence just by paying more.

Some beginning business owners have a tendency to compensate for a lack of employee benefits by cutting their employees in for "a piece of the action." Unless the program is very well thought out, it can be an expensive way to compensate employees.

Many employers in small businesses pay on a commission basis, but this makes no sense unless the employee's performance can influence the sales or net income of the business.

Whatever you decide to pay your employees, and however you intend to structure positions (e.g., part-time, full-time, commissioned, number of hours worked, etc.), you will want to check with a professional to make sure you are complying with all related labor laws and wage restrictions.

FIRING EMPLOYEES

At some point, you or one of your managers will need to fire an employee. It happens in every business. The best approach we have found is to meet with the employee and ask, "Are you having fun?" Almost always when things are not working out with an employee, it is not a fun experience for them, either. Life is too short for anyone to prolong that situation. The thing to do at that point is to make an earnest effort to help the employee move on to an improved situation somewhere else. After they've been fired, employees with whom we have taken that approach thank us when they see us.

It is always a good idea to have thorough records that list any problems with an individual and your attempts to remedy those problems, and which also cover the process you went through leading up to a termination. Unfortunately, we had a manager in the past who drafted a comprehensive explanation of a particular employee's shortcomings and presented that written documentation to the employee during the termination process. This is a really bad idea because it unnecessarily insults and damages the person being fired, and it is overkill. In this case, it caused the terminated individual to become suicidal and resulted in very significant retraining for the manager. However, if the employee being terminated aggressively argues against and challenges the termination decision, at that point you may choose to share that documentation with them.

EMPLOYEE SUPERVISION

We have already covered how paperwork and inventory systems should be in place to minimize the opportunity employees have to steal from the company. You should consider additional common-sense systems regarding employee processes based on your specific operation and the level of employee assigned to any given position.

Over the years, we have discovered that it is especially meaningful to employees to understand they are trusted and are a valuable part of our successful business. When they understand that our company mission is to seek out and take care of the needs of customers, co-workers, and vendors, they have a greater tendency to share our company values. They want to help customers and co-workers. Close supervision is less necessary. And when they are reminded that management is here to provide meaningful and rewarding work in an atmosphere of civility and respect, they feel rewarded for their productivity.

You might be thinking, "This all sounds great on an intellectual level, but don't employees need to be supervised closely so they don't start slacking off more and more over time, getting away with whatever they can?" Actually, no.

This point was driven home to us with all the work-from-home variations we had to implement during the COVID-19 pandemic. More employees were working from home than ever before. Because of how we look for productivity and results—rather than looking for people punching a time clock—we discovered to our surprise and delight that people working from home were frequently even more productive than when they were working in the office. A good way to think about this is that if somebody gets their job completely done in five hours instead of eight, and you are paying them for an eight-hour day, that should be no problem for you as the employer. The key is that they are getting their job 100 percent done. That's what you're really paying them for.

Our managers send out weekly results and goals reports, and in those same reports we have a section available for concerns. This way, we stay on top of productivity and workflow. We simply don't need to worry about folks punching a time clock if they are meeting and exceeding their productivity goals every single week.

You get results from employees whether you're hovering over them or not, as long as they feel empowered to do their job. And not hovering over them signals that you trust them. That is definitely more empowering.

THREE GENERAL PRINCIPLES OF EMPLOYEE PRODUCTIVITY

Whether you work in the same building with your employees or they are working remotely, there are three general principles of productivity:

1. *Get your work done.* (Of course, both the manager and the employee need to agree on goals.)

2. *Be accessible.* If you have employees working remotely, there needs to be a process that allows other people in the company to easily and quickly reach them and get quick responses. If employees are working on site in your office, they need to be available for meetings and other business interactions, as defined by the job description.

3. *Over-communicate.* Employees need to use whatever forms of interaction allow them to frequently and fully express their thoughts and pass along information about their work to other employees and their manager. When you are all working in the same building, this means people need to be available for in-person meetings and quick intercom phone calls, or even stand-up informal meetings in the hallway.

When employees are working remotely, it can be challenging for them to fully communicate their thoughts and input. The big challenge comes when the primary form of communication is written, such as text messages and email. People tend to be more reserved and more precise in their language when they have to put something in writing. "Over-communicating" is a way to avoid miscommunication by omission.

We have found that video meetings, or at least phone meetings, are almost always more complete, quicker, and more productive than exchanging thoughts and opinions about various work projects via email.

THINGS THAT MOTIVATE EMPLOYEES

Your employees are an investment in both time and money. Anything you can do to maximize that investment is always a good idea. It will always be to your benefit as the owner of the company to motivate your employees and get them thinking in the best interests of your customers and the company itself.

Your company mission, USP, and company core values will be foundational and should be reinforced regularly, but there's more that you can roll into your corporate culture to improve motivation.

Things will be different in large companies versus small ones, but employee recognition for a job well done is always a motivator. It may be more personal and involve an unexpected gift card in a mom-and-pop operation, or it may be an employee recognition luncheon with a gift card and public presentation in front of a large gathering of fellow employees.

Intentionally avoiding micromanaging always delivers a welcome job benefit. Employees who feel competent to get their job done right will feel pressured and belittled by managers who are too involved in every little detail of their work. That kind of intrusion also signals that the manager is insecure. Management, *not micro*management, should be the goal.

THE BOTTOM LINE

If you really want to motivate your employees and build a committed team (whether or not you put this in writing), then you should engage your employees in meaningful and rewarding work in an atmosphere of civility and respect.

CHOOSING A NATIONAL COMMANDER
FOR THE CIVIL AIR PATROL

In 2018, Martha was asked if she would be willing to join the Board of Governors of the Civil Air Patrol. As you may know, the Civil Air Patrol was founded during World War II to fly general aviation airplanes over the East Coast to find and report German submarines who were wreaking havoc on the U.S. Merchant Marine. The Civil Air Patrol was enormously effective in stopping the death and destruction caused by the submarines. To this day, the Civil Air Patrol remains the biggest fleet of general aviation airplanes in the world with more than 560 airplanes.

Martha's Board of Governors (BoG) appointment would be a joint appointment of the Secretary of the Air Force and the Civil Air Patrol. Even though Martha and I had little history with the Civil Air Patrol, I encouraged her to accept the appointment because I felt she would grow from the experience.

An example of how she did, in fact, find it a growth experience was the BoG's selection of a new national commander of the Civil Air Patrol. There were three applicants for the position. Martha's observation was that all the applicants were qualified in the fundamentals to a level at which the BoG could not go wrong, but the outstanding applicant was the one who demonstrated superior passion and vision for the mission of the organization.

Her learning experience was that passion and vision were the distinguishing characteristics for a superior leader in nearly every organization.

John

The Civil Air Patrol has the largest fleet of general aviation aircraft in the world—over 560 aircraft.

ATTRACTING AND MOTIVATING EXCEPTIONAL PEOPLE

As our business grew, we began to have a need for high-level managers with specialized skills. It was apparent we needed to learn how to attract that level of manager. We knew that we needed to provide them meaningful and rewarding work in an atmosphere of civility and respect just as we did for all other employees. The difference in this case would be, what would be meaningful and rewarding work to these high-level people? One of the advantages we have is that we teach flying, and aviation is a subject for which many people have a great passion. This makes our company very attractive to them. In the case of these high-level people with a passion for flying, incorporating flying into their work makes the work meaningful and rewarding for them. As time progressed, we realized that focusing on the specific needs and drives of these achievers would be very beneficial to both us and them.

When we first started selling videos to our customers, we understood we were in the video business, and realized we would need managers with video expertise. Fortunately, we had met David Jackson whom our friend, Phil Boyer of ABC, had recruited from Hollywood. Dave was an aviation enthusiast and pilot as well as being a movie producer/director who was extraordinarily knowledgeable and competent in the video and film business. We had watched Dave conduct an audio "sweetening" session for Phil and were very impressed with his knowledge and attention to detail. When Dave came to King Schools as our Vice President, Video

Production, his background and skills benefited the company enormously. We were especially appreciative of Dave's civil and respectful treatment of everyone he dealt with. As we watched Dave manage his department and his other relationships smoothly and competently, we developed a deep respect for his civil manner and managerial skills. We eventually asked Dave to head up the company with the title of president. He eventually also became our CEO.

Dave's competence and ethical nature allowed him to recruit people of similar caliber. One of Dave's recruits was Barry Knuttila, who was also an aviation enthusiast and a pilot. Barry had previously headed up a software development program and initially came on board as our Vice-President, Technology. Barry reported directly to Dave, and when Dave retired, Barry replaced Dave as the CEO. Over time Barry's software knowledge and expertise became increasingly important as we moved to both marketing and delivering our courses online. We realized that the products we sold were enabled by software and software represented a significant amount of the value we provided to our customers. Barry has become a stock-owning partner with us in the business, is an instructor on the videos teaching our customers, and has become rated to fly our small company jet, the Falcon 10. He has guided the company with great insight, kindness and wisdom, and an even demeanor, and his results reflect his competence.

John and Martha

Dave in the Debonair: Flying has been important to
Dave Jackson for his entire adult life.

Martha and Barry: Barry Knuttila and Martha enjoy flying together as a well-functioning crew in the Falcon 10.

9

THE POWER OF NON-MANIPULATIVE SELLING

You, as an entrepreneur, will want to learn the fundamentals of sales. An important thing to learn about sales is that a successful salesperson is not "slick" or manipulative; a successful salesperson is knowledgeable and skilled in the fundamentals of how to seek out and take care of a customer's needs.

Non-manipulative selling is built on the foundation of what we call "TNT," the acronym we discussed in Chapter Two. It stands for Trust (or Trustworthy), Needs, and Triumph with a solution. Below is a re-cap of the principles, but we've gone a little deeper.

TRUST

It is very difficult to accomplish anything through other people unless you have established the element of trust with them. A person trusts someone who they believe:

- Respects them
- Has their interests at heart: When it is outwardly apparent that you have the best interests of your clients at heart, you will more likely be seen as being trustworthy. You should be saying and doing things that demonstrate that you care about your clients, prospects, and their experiences with your products or services and the problems they solve.
- Is predictable: when people can count on you to make truthful promises and follow through. This is critical to your being seen as predictable.
- Plays by fair rules: When you are seen as someone who plays by fair rules, people are far more inclined to count on you. That means you deliver on promises and regularly do the right thing, and even over-deliver whenever you possibly can.

When you show your customers that they can trust you, your customer reviews will almost entirely be five-star because you deliver a noteworthy, positive customer experience.

NEEDS

To be effective at sales, it is important to know your customers' needs so you can meet (and surpass) those needs. It is most effective to start your contemplation of the market by identifying a customer need or want that you can fulfill ethically and profitably, and that should be the offer you make in your sales process.

Of course, you'll want to remember that needs are personal. Clients should be able to trust that the money they give to a person or company will result in their own needs being fulfilled.

Researching and understanding customer needs is the first key step in the sales process, including asking questions when you're talking with clients and prospects. This habit will help you understand the needs or wants you can fulfill.

The next step is:

TRIUMPH WITH A SOLUTION

The solution you present needs to be tailored to the customer's situation. You can use the answers you get when asking about customer needs to pick the best possible offer and present it in the right way.

Develop a mental checklist regarding your offering before you describe your solution to your customer. A way to remember to get everything into your explanation is to think in terms of "FAB":

- Features: Describe the elements of your product or service. These are the hard facts about what you offer: e.g., factory specifications regarding size, weight, power usage, length of warranty, etc.
- Advantages: Explain why the features make your product better than competing products. Is it smaller, lighter, more stylish, etc.? An advantage also might be finishing a task more quickly, or saving money.

- Benefits: Answer the customer's question—"So what?"—about the advantages by taking the explanation a step further. Benefits solve problems for the customer and are often emotional. They are the payoff to the customer. Maybe the payoff is getting more time to spend with family. Maybe your solution gives them more money to spend on eating out or traveling, or whatever they choose. The payoff reaches customers as a good feeling in their gut. Those feelings, those payoffs, are the benefits

You'll want to pay close attention to all the customer's stated needs and then repeat them back. You should not only find the solution that fulfills all their needs, but should also describe how your solution meets each of those needs. Repeating their needs builds trust because it proves you were listening and not just pushing ahead on your own agenda. What may be an obvious solution to you is almost always less obvious to your prospect, because if they knew everything you know they would have bought your goods or services already.

Listening closely to customer needs might lead to you offering something different from what you had originally planned when you first met them and guessed their needs and wants. In order to triumph with the right solution, you need to be flexible and offer the best solution under the current circumstances.

And, of course, your prospect must be willing and able to pay for your solution.

SUCCESSFUL SELLING

Just closing a sale is not the primary indicator of an expert salesperson. Success is all about your ability to find and deliver the right solution for your client. That ability is the key indicator of your expertise as a salesperson. You must genuinely have the interests of your client at heart.

Study and research regarding your product or service is useful because it will help you be able to explain the features, advantages, and benefits of all you have to offer, in a way that covers what the customer needs.

As a successful salesperson, you will want to remember that everyone in life, including your customer, is thinking in terms of one thing: WIIFM ("What's in it for me?").

At some point, every good salesperson thinks, *I wish I could just get inside their head and know what they're thinking.* We can tell you what they're thinking: They're thinking, *WIIFM.* (We pronounce it "wiffem.") As we said, it stands for **What's In It For Me?** As you engage, you should constantly be thinking about presenting your offering in a way that helps the customer see what is in it for them.

CUSTOMERS DON'T BUY WHEN THEY DON'T PERCEIVE A SOLUTION

Even if you think you've addressed WIIFM and explained the features, advantages, and benefits, if the prospect doesn't perceive a solution, they won't buy. Usually, people try to be polite and will say something like, "I need to think about it." But typically the non-sale comes down to one of several possibilities: Maybe you haven't listened well and haven't offered the right solution. And even if you have listened well and you are offering the right solution, it's possible you haven't communicated that solution well enough.

Beyond those basics, there are a few more factors that can stop a sale, and these indicate that one of the earlier steps isn't complete. You won't make the sale if customers don't trust you or if they don't need what you're selling.

This is a point of exasperation for some salespeople, and out of frustration they may turn to something you should never do: the "power close." Forcing the sale, even if you believe in your heart that the offer is right for your prospect, has too many repercussions for that hard close to be worthwhile.

Forcing the sale erodes the element of trust. The result, in most cases, is that the harder you push, the more they pull away. And even if you do close the sale, they'll be looking for ways to get out of the commitment—and they certainly won't be buying from you again in the future or telling others they should buy from you.

WHAT IS "SELLING"?

This is a good time to define what we mean when we talk about "selling." Anytime someone buys something, a "sale" has been made. That sale can be made one-on-one in person, or via the web, or on the telephone.

The sales process can be done personally and conversationally, or indirectly on the internet, or through email or postal mail, or through TV or magazine ads. For clarity, in this chapter we'll focus on techniques related to personal sales interactions, and we'll refer to that as "sales" and "selling." In the next chapter, when we discuss using media or technology as the means of communication, we'll refer to that as "response (or direct) marketing." With either approach, the fundamental truth is that selling is a process of seeking out and taking care of other people's needs.

One of the basic principles of entrepreneurship—especially sales—is that everyone should be better off because of our relationship. That includes benefiting the customer as well as making a profit. It is essential to follow that policy not only for short-term profit but also, especially, for the long-term health of the business.

THE SURPRISING BUSINESS PRACTICE WE USE PROFITABLY TODAY

As you can see, we have strong feelings that our businesses must maintain trustworthiness by avoiding anything that involves less-than-respectful treatment of our customers. We feel so strongly about this that we published this mission statement, which we posted on our website and at the entrance to our building:

> *"King Schools is in the business of providing an outstanding customer experience to users of our aviation education and related products, sold through ethical and responsible marketing. It is the goal of King Schools to do good things for people and to succeed by seeking out and taking care of the needs of our customers, fellow workers, and vendors."*
>
> **— King Schools Mission Statement**

As customers of numerous businesses, we had both come to dislike telemarketing. It has become more annoying over the years with autodialers and recordings and fake caller I.D. info, so after countless bad experiences receiving all kinds of rude and deceptive sales calls, we had no interest in becoming yet another company that marketed this way. Telemarketing was a non-starter for us and the management team at King Schools knew it.

That's why the takeaway we gathered from a marketing seminar Martha attended created so much discussion. At the seminar, she learned that if you have a good direct-mail marketing campaign and you follow it up with a good telemarketing campaign, you can increase your sales by as much as 50 percent.

Wow! With numbers like that, we needed to see if there was some way we could do telemarketing that would be respectful to our valued customers and prospects.

As with any good training seminar, you ponder and rehash the content and look through your notes for a day or two when you get home. This seminar was the focus of dinner and evening conversations in the King household, and the telemarketing claim was both discomforting and exciting. We were compelled to at least explore telemarketing possibilities, even though we didn't know how we could do it and remain consistent with our business values.

At our next management team meeting, to the surprise of everyone else in the room, we brought up the subject of telemarketing. We explained that we wanted to know what their thoughts were and see if anyone on our talented team had an idea about how we might approach telemarketing ethically.

We weren't surprised that there had been a number of contacts to our company from people wishing to sell telemarketing services and training, which never got past our gatekeepers. But now that we had brought it up, it turned out that one of the people trying to get King Schools into telemarketing was a pilot. When he made his original pitch and asked to speak to us, our employee told him, "The Kings have made it clear that they're not interested in telemarketing." He had replied, "Well, that's just because they don't know about classy and ethical telemarketing."

They talked for a little longer and the call wasn't pushy or anything like our stereotypical negative view of telemarketing, but it still didn't get past our gatekeeper. However, because the person was a pilot and had an interesting angle and polite demeanor based on an ethical approach, our team member had saved the contact information and was able to reach him. We started talking with our new friend, the classy telemarketer.

We learned that the classy approach to telemarketing requires some key elements:

1. You explain who you are.
2. You explain what the call is about.
3. You ask permission to continue the call.

Here's how it can go:

"Hi, I'm Bill Jones. I'm a flight instructor with King Schools. Do you have time to talk about your flying?"

This has identified who you are, what the call is about, and has asked permission to continue the call.

We have an advantage over many companies using telemarketing. Asking a pilot if they have time to talk about flying gets an immediate "yes" almost every single time. And because our team members live our company values, the conversations become excited, friendly, and interactive. Not only do most pilots absolutely love talking about flying, sometimes they are so engaged in the conversation that our team members have difficulty wrapping up the phone call. Needless to say, sales have increased.

We don't call these folks "telemarketers," or even "outbound sales folks," like many companies do. We call them our "personal sales team," because there is nothing more personal than two pilots talking on the phone together while trying to make one person's flying better and easier. It demonstrates our respect for both parties to the conversation.

MANIPULATIVE VS. NON-MANIPULATIVE SELLING

In the 1990s, when we developed our DVD video courses for entrepreneurs, we titled our sales course "Non-manipulative Selling for Sales Growth." Today, every King Schools employee involved in sales takes this video course before interacting with King Schools clients and prospects.

The goal of all selling is to change a person's behavior, but you want to do it in an honest, non-manipulative, straight-forward way.

We define "manipulative selling" as a sales process having some or all of these characteristics:

- False rapport
- Hard sell

- Hiding information or delaying the reveal of information
- Containing one or more unfair or deceptive elements to the customer

Non-manipulative selling is open, straightforward, honest, and fair to the customer—and never degrading to the salesperson. The sales process should be viewed as helping people overcome the fear that prevents them from doing what they really do want to do.

THE BEST RESPONSE TO A "NO SALE" — UNDERSTAND, DON'T TRY TO OVERCOME

Since a hard close and arguing won't make the sale, your fallback position should be to ask questions in order to understand. You need to understand how to better adjust or describe your offer so it actually meets the needs of your customer. In many sales training courses, people call this "overcoming objections." We don't. In the minds of many people, the term "overcoming objections" is nearly synonymous with the concept of overpowering the customer's objections, and that frame of mind won't get you where you need to be.

After you review the customer's perceptions, their needs, and your proposed solution, you should make adjustments to your offer or how you present it. Ultimately, you need to understand the objections. In the long run, even if you aren't able to sell to this prospect today, if you truly understand their objections you can be ready for those same objections from future prospects by adjusting your presentation or redesigning your products or services, or both.

A POWERFUL TOOL THAT REMOVES THE FEAR OF RISK

If your customer's objections seem to be centered around the risk being too high for them, there's something you can do to minimize that risk—or perhaps eliminate it altogether. You can provide a guarantee. In fact, our advice is, "Make the very best guarantee you can afford."

When you make your presentation and ask for their business (make your close), you want them to take action. When you eliminate the risk by giving them a guarantee, you remove fear and give them the freedom to take action.

At King Schools, we have employed the money-back guarantee for years and it has worked incredibly well for us. For one of our programs, we even came up with a better offer than money back.

In the early days, when our classes were delivered on video tapes to flight instructors around the country who used them to teach their learning pilots, we used to take the information for a credit card payment but did not charge the card for sixty days. We structured our guarantee this way because we knew that flight instructors didn't make much money and would need help paying for the video courses. This deferred payment allowed the flight instructors to advertise and hold their first class using our videos to teach their students, and to earn a profit from their class *before* we processed the credit card payment. Charging the credit card only after the program was a proven success that resulted in a truly risk-free approach to buying our class videos. The instructors' first class paid for the tapes.

Initially, this was a bit of a gamble for us. We didn't know how many of our customers would keep and pay for the video course because it paid off for them. In the end, we had under 1 percent returns, so our guarantee was a huge success!

These days we have upped our game and now have a triple guarantee that you can find right on our website. It puts prospective customers at ease and makes the buying decision so low-risk for them, there's practically no reason for them to hesitate if they're in the market for one of our courses.

Our "money-back triple guarantee" is:

1. If you're not completely satisfied with the course, return it within thirty days for a prompt, friendly refund.
2. Your course will be up to date with the latest FAA knowledge requirements.
3. If you fail your FAA test within one year of purchase, get your money back *and* you keep the course!

We also—while it's not directly a part of our money-back guarantee—allow our customers to access the course(s) they bought forever. We always keep our courses current and if they want to retake a course as a refresher, they always have access to the most current version of that course. This makes the second part of our guarantee even stronger.

THE SINGLE BIGGEST FAILURE

The single biggest failure a salesperson can make—and it happens all the time—is the failure to request action. This happens because the seller completely understands their own offering—they know how worthwhile their offer is and how obvious the value should be, so they make their case, present their features, advantages, and benefits, and then expect the sale. The truth is, it's incredibly rare for a customer to just say, out of the blue, "I'll take it." You almost always have to *ask* the customer to take action.

The great news is that it usually only takes a little nudge—a simple question to overcome natural inertia. Just ask the prospect to buy what you're offering.

THE PSYCHOLOGY OF THE CLOSE

The Question

When it's closing time, you need to ask a question. Remember to be consistent with your personal speaking style. These examples should give you a starting point, but feel free to adjust or combine these options until you find the question that works best for you personally:

- Does this make sense to you?
- Does what we've talked about appear to be a solution that meets your needs?

In response to a prospect saying, "I'm just not sure":

- What do you need to know in order to make a decision today?
- If we answer this concern of yours, would you be able to make a decision today?

If you're very far along in the conversation and the prospect seems to be on the verge of buying, you can ask:

- Would you like to use a credit card to pay for this **today?**

When asking any of these questions, you need to state your question simply and directly, then wait for their answer. It's almost always far less effective to give the prospect several choices as part of your question. This is why you don't ask, "Would you like to pay by check, credit card, or PayPal?" People have a lot to think about and they need a single question that simply asks them to make the buying decision.

If you keep it simple by asking if they want to pay by credit card and they reply, "Can I use PayPal instead?," you know you have made the sale. Now you just need to work out the details about how to take their payment.

Silence Matters

The other thing you must do after you have asked them to buy is to be quiet. Don't interrupt the silence. Always wait for the customer to speak first, because they will either state an objection or they will buy. If *you* speak first, it would only be because you are guessing why they are hesitating, and unless you are truly psychic you'll almost always guess wrong.

Objections Are a Good Thing

If doing sales is relatively new to you, it's helpful to realize that objections are an indicator that the prospect is participating in the sales process as an interested party. They are not just politely listening with no intention of buying. Objections are the efforts of the prospect to make sure your proposal is truly in their best interest. A disinterested party won't slow things down by offering an objection. They'll just say no.

When You Get an Objection

When you get an objection, the most important thing to do is make sure you understand it. If you aren't absolutely sure you fully understand their objection, start with a question like, "How do you mean that?" Then, to make absolutely sure you do understand, repeat the objection back to the customer. But don't stop there—you need to ask if there are any more objections.

Answer Those Objections

You need to propose a solution that directly addresses the core of the objection. It would also be especially effective to shift the risk of the perceived problem to yourself. If it's possible, you might consider saying, "If this becomes a problem, we will make it right." On the other hand, if the problem is related to price, it will help to explain the quality, service, savings, and convenience of your offering. You should try to help your prospect fully understand that your offer is not simply a commodity. It is unique and cannot be interchanged with other products or services that are offered by competitors, and the offer cannot be obtained elsewhere for less money.

When Objections Don't Make Sense

Sometimes you might get an objection that makes absolutely no sense to you. When this happens, the stated objection is usually just a tool the prospect is using because they have some other objection they do not want to disclose. Perhaps stating the real objection may embarrass them or someone in their company. It's also possible that they may not trust you.

When you are met with an objection that doesn't make sense and you don't know the real objection, you need to deal with the stated objection while trying to decipher what the true objection is. As you are addressing the stated objection, slip in the question, "Is there any other reason you feel this might not work for you?" You may even need to ask this question a few times to get a reasonable response.

OTHER CONSIDERATIONS FOR SOME ENTREPRENEURS

Depending on your business model, your sales process could be largely marketing-oriented, and the one-to-one sales process described here will not be a part of your everyday operations. If that's the case, the next chapter on direct-response marketing will be a great resource for you. Just keep in mind that practically every business will need some form of personal sales process, even if it's just to establish relationships with vendors, your bank, or other types of partners.

If your business model does incorporate person-to-person selling as a part of regular operations, you will likely need to have some best-practice concepts in place for handling things like sales management, recruiting, training, motivation, and tools for telephone sales.

WHO IS THE BUYER?

When you have a business customer you would like to sell to but has no existing relationship with the company, the first thing you need to do is find out who the buyer at the company will be. That's often not the CEO, so you need to do a little bit of investigative research as you work to make your appointment. When you call the company to get the appointment, you should obviously be respectful to the receptionist or screener. Not only is this the right thing to do, but you also need their help. The goal is not to get past them but to solicit their help in connecting you with the right person.

When you reach the person who has the authority to purchase, or their direct assistant who makes appointments for them, you should be respectful of their time and attention. Start by giving them full information. Tell them who you are, what the call is about, how long the phone call will take, and convey the benefits of talking about this subject. If you want an in-person meeting, tell them how long the actual meeting will take, and suggest a day and time for that meeting.

TELEPHONE SALES

If your business model relies on sales conducted over the phone, you definitely have a challenge because of how abusive the telesales business has become. Everything from robocalls to car-warranty scams has people on guard against any callers who might be trying to sell something. Our natural reaction to someone proposing telemarketing to us was an immediate "No!" Of course, we have a very successful telemarketing department today because we learned about ethical telemarketing and how to do it.

Even if you don't sell pilot courses, you should follow the formula of identifying yourself and your company right up front and asking for permission to continue the conversation.

SALES MANAGEMENT

Managing salespeople involves the process of recruiting, training, motivating, measuring and controlling, and respectfully deselecting.

- *Recruiting* is a matter of finding people who have a passion for the subject your company is involved in. You will want to find people who like working with others and who are listeners. They should be eager to listen to company management of course, but they should also be eager to listen to what customers and prospects are saying.

- *Training* should include information about your products and services, but don't stop there. By the time you are hiring additions to your sales staff, you should already have a solid understanding of what your customer needs are, and this must be a part of your sales training. Of course, the other necessary component is that your sales team must understand non-manipulative selling.

- *Motivating* your sales professionals is done in a number of ways. In almost every case, salespeople earn a base salary plus a commission based on their sales. Beyond that, there are incentive programs, company-recognition programs, and bonus programs based on sales numbers and achieving or surpassing targets.

- *Measuring and controlling* your sales team and your sales process is critical, since salary and bonuses are based on sales performance figures. These figures should always include some sort of metrics such as sales per hour or sales per week.

- And, of course, the sales managers in your company will need to *respectfully deselect people who are not performing*. The term "not performing" has two important definitions. The first definition is what you would expect: salespeople who are not making sufficient sales to justify their employment. But the second definition is just as important, if not more so—you should always separate salespeople from your company who do not subscribe to your company's core values.

It is an unfortunate reality that, many times, salespeople who exhibit unethical behavior, rudeness, or other negative personality traits, but who have a really impressive set of sales numbers, will be retained by some companies. This signals to other salespeople that they can ignore the rules and still make their salary and bonuses, and it signals to other employees that you don't take your company values seriously. Allowing a salesperson to be a jerk and still keep their job if they sell enough is a sure-fire way to tick off customers and prospects, and it will move your company toward failure.

THE MAIN THING A GREAT SALESPERSON DOES

There is a lot to selling, but the primary thing a great salesperson does is to help a prospect overcome their fear that prevents them from buying something they really do want. A great salesperson provides information from a trustworthy individual and company in the form of a triumphant solution to a customer's needs.

LEARNING HOW TO SELL AT A YOUNG AGE

When I was fourteen, my parents decided to drive me into Indianapolis from our country gas station to attend a dealer training school. My fellow meeting attendees were all men who owned service station dealerships. My father was concerned that I would be too mouthy. Obviously, that was a possibility, because I was being sent off to attend sales training. So as they dropped me off at the hotel where the training was to take place, my dad gave me some advice. "John, none of these people want the advice of a fourteen-year-old. You should just keep your mouth shut and listen." Listen, I did.

When I came home to our gas station and restaurant, I began selling oil changes with the suggestion that the people could have lunch in our restaurant while they had their oil changed. My sales efforts made a noticeable increase in the revenue of the family business. Employees had to be added to handle the additional work.

I had learned how to frame the sales pitch in terms of our customers' needs. Plus, I had learned to put my mouthiness that folks were concerned about to good use at an early age.

John

USING SCIENTIFIC MARKETING TO GENERATE SALES

You will, as an entrepreneur, find direct-response marketing to be a tool that will benefit you greatly. Direct-response marketing, also sometimes known more simply as direct marketing or response marketing, is communication sent directly to a customer you expect to respond directly to you.

Direct-response marketing solicits a specific action such as to buy a specific thing, go to a specific web page to take a free course, or make a phone call. You want each prospect to take an action you can track and measure. You want to be able to accurately quantify how many people respond to each of your marketing investments so you know how to proceed in the future.

While salesmanship is one on one, direct-response marketing is salesmanship multiplied. It is often referred to as "scientific marketing," because you have created a repeatable process that generates a measurable response. It is an effective way to sell products or services that cannot be sold economically one on one.

The elements of direct-response marketing are:

- *A clear and definite offer*: The recipient of the offer needs to have a clear understanding of what they will get and what they have to do to get it.
- *All the information necessary to make a decision*: The recipient needs to know the features, advantages, and benefits of what you are selling.
- *The motivation to buy*: The recipient needs to know why they should buy *now* (emotional appeals help here).
- *A call to action*: The potential buyer must understand that they are expected to take immediate action.
- *A response device*: The recipient must be provided with all the tools to conveniently respond and make a purchase.

Direct-response marketing can take advantage of direct mail, marketing emails, magazine ads with a coupon, an 800 number, a URL, Google ad service, social media, and more.

One of the most important things to understand about direct-response marketing is that it is a scientific approach to marketing when you use split-testing properly. It is equally important to understand that split-testing is a powerful tool you can use with direct-response marketing. Split-testing lets you precisely measure which of two ways a customer prefers to buy. Failure to use split-testing when you have a direct-response marketing campaign is throwing away money, because you have no idea if some small, simple change might increase your profits.

DIRECT-RESPONSE MARKETING IS TOPS — BRAND-AWARENESS MARKETING IS NOT

Over the years in our many business efforts, we have always used direct-response marketing, as opposed to what is known as "brand-awareness marketing." As you can probably guess from our earlier chapters, we are only comfortable investing when there is a measurable return. And specifically, with marketing, we only invest in advertising efforts when we can measure the results of our marketing investment. It is difficult for most entrepreneurs to measure the results from brand marketing. Consequently, direct-response marketing is a safer investment.

Disclaimer: It is theoretically possible that a large, multi-billion-dollar company can gain measurable market share by spending millions on something like a Super Bowl commercial that stars a very famous celebrity, but those expenditures are well beyond the entrepreneur target market of this book.

DIRECT-RESPONSE MARKETING USES MANY OF THE SAME ELEMENTS AS PERSONAL SALES

In the last chapter, we discussed tools used by salespeople during the selling process. Many of these tools can be used in the absence of direct human interaction. For example, TNT (gain Trust, find customer Needs, and Triumph with a solution) is a solid approach to selling, regardless of the medium you are using—whether it's in magazine ads, on video ads, in social media, or in email marketing. Obviously, some of the things you would say in a personal conversation would need to be adjusted to reach your typical customer in other media. In business these days, it's possible that some marketing professionals would call your image of your customer an "avatar."

Avatar

If you're unfamiliar with the concept of an avatar in a business context, an avatar is a fictional person who represents your typical customer. Let's say you are in the home hardware business. As you develop research about your target-market average buyer, you may develop a mental image of your buyer that you might come to think of as a person. Let's call that person your "avatar." You may come to discover that, say, the average age of your customer is thirty-eight years old. They primarily live in the Southwest. They are male with hobbies like camping and woodworking. They love the TV show *Home Improvement*. And they consider themselves upper middle class. Knowing this about a "typical" customer, a business might create a drawing of a guy and give him a name—maybe "Tim." Then put those bullet points on the drawing of Tim. As direct-response ad campaigns are developed, the marketing team would ask themselves, "What websites would Tim visit? What YouTube videos would Tim watch? What offer would motivate Tim to take action?"

Most companies have a male and female avatar, and some companies have four or more total avatars. They are just an internal tool used to help businesses design their products, services, marketing campaign descriptions, and their call-to-action offers. An avatar should be considered a tool to help you find lists of people who might be interested in your products, and can also help you develop a good starting offer. Avatars should always be adjusted as you gather new information about your target market(s). You should never discount a product, service, offer idea, or marketing channel just because it does not fit perfectly with your avatar.

In our example of a 38-year-old male who likes *Home Improvement* reruns, if you discover one of your product offerings is especially popular with twenty-five-year-old females, consider developing a new avatar named "Jessica." You can make tailored offers to her and make separate ongoing offers to Tim.

ELEMENTS OF YOUR RESPONSE ADS

Ad Elements and the Call to Action

When you think back to the person-to-person sales process, first there is the element of a discussion, where questions are asked and the presentation and offer are presented and refined, and then there is the ask. Similarly, with direct-response advertising you have an ad that must contain a presentation of your product or service and a call to action. In addition to these two components, the primary elements of your response ad include the creative content, the audience, and the offer.

- *Creative* – The creative aspect of your non-video ads will be the layout, the look and feel, graphics, a picture of the product in use, and the text. Of course, the call to action (CTA) is included as well. With video ads you need no more than three main points of information in a sixty-second video ad and only one or two key points in a thirty-second ad. As in traditional salesmanship, always close with a single call to action. Don't give viewers too many options or they won't take action.

- *Audience* – Your audience will be a group of people you pick based on your avatar. You might reach them in an industry magazine, a Facebook group, a YouTube video ad, or an email list. Your target audience members will eventually be current and former customers, as well as prospects who are participating someplace where you can pay to reach out to them. The goal is to add as many people as possible to email lists you own and that those people have voluntarily joined. You will want to entice them to your list with attractive offers, sometimes even with free offers. Folks who respond to free offers and then find they like your product or service can generate substantial lifetime value.

- *The Offer* – Whatever you are selling, your description must be interesting to your target market. It should be compelling and easily understood. Your call to action should be the "how-to" part of the ad that encourages action to purchase, or some other action that is consistent with your customer flow. Realize that the customer wants to know: "What do I get? What must I do to get it?"

- The Call to Action – Your call to action isn't always a request to purchase, although it might be. It could also be a request for someone to watch a video, read a blog post, or download an e-book. The key is that the call to action *must* be measurable. This way you can determine that the $450 you spent on a certain social media ad generated 1,634 views of your free video training. With a little further tracking, you can discover that 86 percent of those who watched your free video bought $245 worth of video classes within thirty days.

INVESTMENTS THAT PAY OFF BIG

Over the years, we have made quite a few adjustments in our ad campaigns to try and get the best possible response. In any business, you can work to improve various aspects of your ads and see more sales as a result, but we have found that some improvements are much more effective than others. What follows is a set of general guidelines based on our experiences over the years:

Creative Improvements

If you improve the look and layout of your ad or if you improve the cinematic quality of your video ad, you may see an improvement in bottom-line sales of something like 10 percent.

Audience Improvements

If you spend time with search engine optimization (SEO), use audience research tools available for social media, or partner with organizations (like industry email newsletters) that have better email lists, and (as a result) you find better-defined target markets, your bottom-line sales could improve by 100 percent or more.

Change the Offer Itself

If you improve your offer or satisfaction guarantee to make it as appealing as possible to your audience, you can see the biggest growth numbers. This is where we have experienced increased sales of over 1,000 percent.

With this in mind, when you've created an ad campaign and made sales, the next step is always to make adjustments in order to see if there's a way to increase sales. In our experience, you will make the most progress by changing your offer first. Our strongest advice is to always make the best guarantee you can afford.

A PRACTICE THAT ERODES TRUST

Something we see quite a bit is a teaser offer with a push to go somewhere else for "more information." Almost every time, that "more information" turns out to be a longer, more detailed, hard sales pitch with more things to buy than what was suggested in the beginning. This prominent online "bait and switch" approach is a bad practice that's been around for decades. You will not likely build a successful business with happy repeat customers using this trust-destroying approach.

When you're an honest entrepreneur, there's no need for any kind of heavy-handed approach. If you started your business in the very beginning by researching what you could sell at a profit—something that solves a problem and for which people are willing to pay—an appropriate explanation of your offer and a clear CTA (call to action) will make a very reliable and systematic sale.

A HANDFUL OF SIMPLE AD ELEMENTS TO BUILD CREDIBILITY

Years ago, placing a medium-to-large ad in a magazine, newspaper, or on TV would automatically give you credibility with your target market because those kinds of ads were expensive, and the publications vetted them. Today, unfortunately, the most untrustworthy kinds of people can buy ads that make them seem bigger and more trustworthy than they are.

Be sure to include a URL in your ad so people can do a little investigative research on your company if they are so inclined. A business phone number, especially a toll-free 800 number, adds credibility. And of course, a physical business address adds further credibility. Each of these items included in an ad will build your credibility and help prospective buyers be more comfortable making their purchase decision.

WIIFM MATTERS JUST AS MUCH IN DIRECT-RESPONSE MARKETING AS IN DIRECT SALES

In Chapter Ten, we talked about how so many salespeople wish they could get inside the heads of people they talk to so they could know what they are thinking, and we said they're thinking, "WIIFM" ("What's in it for me?"). In the personal communication selling process, you can ask questions and discuss elements of your offer to make sure you address the WIIFM questions, but since advertising and marketing require you to create your presentation in advance, you need to consider what your WIIFM answers should be.

Elements that answer WIIFM in ads include:

- Price/payment terms
- Guarantee
- Premium or free gift
- Sweepstakes entry
- Shipping terms
- Time limit
- Charter offer
- Special to a certain group
- Get-a-friend program

If your business is offering products or services that could be provided to customers over time, you can structure a "negative offer" that allows someone to sign up for a subscription that they can cancel at any time, or return their unwanted subscription item for a credit. An old example of this is the book-of-the-month club. You paid a regular monthly fee and then you received a new book each month. If you didn't like the book, you could return it for a credit. Now, before you start laughing and think to yourself, *That kind of thing would never work today*, I'll stop you and say, not only does this work today, the biggest audio book provider in the world, Audible, is using this same business model.

Audible's monthly subscription rate gives you one audible book download per month. You can collect credits and then download several audio books. If you want more books than you have credits for, you can download more books and pay a reduced rate for the extras. You can even "return" audio books you don't like for a credit and buy a different audio book. This is a solid business model.

Payments, Premiums, and Guarantees That Address WIIFM:

Payment terms

- Single payment
- Installment payments
- Buy four, get one free

Premiums

- Buy course and get [insert number] mini courses free
- Free gift with order over $450

Guarantee — make the very best guarantee you can afford

- Free trial
- Satisfaction with return privilege
- Get results or get your money back

AD COPY THAT SELLS

Writing good advertising copy for print, web ads, or video is a topic that's taught in colleges and universities and more online ad classes than you can count. That course content could merit a book of its own. We don't have that level of deep dive planned for you here, but we've got the basics outlined to give you a good, solid start with your ad copy.

Your ad copy should be:

- Clear, simple, straightforward, direct
- Active rather than passive voice

Personal, talks about the reader (use the word "you" and not "most people," as most people won't be buying your product or service but this reader/listener might be)

Ads and their copy must support your style. John and Martha King are:

- Informal
- Unpretentious
- Folksy
- Fun

Be sure to use the tone and vocabulary that is right for you.

Very early on, you must give people reasons to continue to read. Think WIIFM. Give a benefit so it resonates.

Just like with person-to-person selling, ads must contain all the information necessary to make a decision and move ahead with the call to action and/or purchase. As we stated in Chapter Nine, that information includes:

- Features—what is it?
- Advantages—answers the "so what?" of the features
- Benefits—answers the "so what?" of the advantages

YOUR GRAPHICS

Graphics are an important part of every still and video ad. Make sure they meet all these following key points: Good-looking graphics can help establish trust, but that's not the primary use of graphics. They must support the objective of the ad. Also, despite what a graphic artist might think looks edgy or cool, your graphics must be readable.

Ads have to capture the attention of the target market quickly and that means the primary visual impact of the ad needs to connect quickly. Once that visual connection is made and you get the prospect to look a little more closely and pay more attention, they should see the ad "unfold" and deliver more information in the proper order for the reader or viewer. We refer to this as how "scannable" an ad is. Your still ads must take advantage of first- and second-order scannables. For instance, high-order scannables are the first thing your eyes go to when you look at an ad.

- First order: dominant graphics photos, headlines
- Second order: subheads, captions, underlining
- Third order: body copy

Another thing you'll remember from our sales chapter is REMUS, and, of course, the REMUS test should also be applied to your ad graphics. Graphics should be:

- Relevant
- Engaging
- Memorable
- Unexpected
- Simple

VIDEO ADS

With video ads, things are a little different. The best general formula for a video ad is to start with a hook that causes the viewer to stop and pay attention. Immediately after the attention-getting hook, make a promise of a benefit for watching the video. For example, if your target market is photographers, you might have a hook like, "Is flash photography dead?" That might be followed by a strong promise like, "In the next fifty seconds, you'll learn how a new lighting technique outshines flash photos every time." A simple, effective video ad formula is:

- Hook
- Promise
- Inform and teach (demonstrate if possible)
- Show examples of "Wow!" images
- Close with a single call to action

REAL WORLD SPLIT TEST (A/B) EXPERIMENTS

Our Case Study and Scientific Proof of Concept

In 1991, we were delivering ground-school courses on VHS tapes. In addition to magazine ads, one of our marketing channels was direct mail to new pilots and student pilots. We got lists of these newly registered student pilots from the FAA and we would send a direct-response marketing piece to them via U.S. mail. (These lists are no longer available from the FAA.)

It's important to know that the market we were in was declining.

Airplane sales in those years had dropped dramatically. And while new student pilot registrations with the FAA weren't down as much as airplane sales, they were still declining noticeably. We were working hard to leverage the tools available to us in direct-response marketing to grow our pilot training business in a shrinking market.

Spoiler alert: We did it!

Working along the lines of best practices of the day, we prepared a marketing package that we mailed to the names on the lists we got from the FAA. Inside the main mailing envelope were a number of printed pieces designed to describe who King Schools was and what we had to offer. Inside, people would find a business reply envelope, a letter, and a brochure describing who the Kings are and inviting people to "Meet the Kings." In order to make this a scientific split test, we created an identical package with all the same items except the letter. Instead of receiving a letter communicating our offer, potential customers received a VHS video which contained the communication and offer.

To Make Things Scientific

One of the critical factors in creating a viable scientific test is that you must plan to send your offer to thousands of people so you have a sufficient number of responses to be a valid test. That means you should design the test so that you can expect to have at least fifty responses on each side of the test. Another critical factor is that you can only make one change as you split the list for testing. In other words, you shouldn't change the name of the package at the same time you are changing two or three of the elements in the package or the addressee locations. Just start with a nice big list, make two separate packages with one difference between them, and mail each package to every other name on the list (an A/B split), and see how the two sets compare.

We had two versions of our offer. Thousands of people got the flat mailer with the letter, while an equal number of people got the VHS package in a "Jiffy" mailer envelope. The flat package with no VHS tape had a cost to mail of $486 per one thousand people. The VHS tape version cost us $2,316 per one thousand people. The cost was considerably more for the VHS tape version of the offer—almost five times as much. But cost is only part of the equation. The more important consideration was the contribution to the bottom-line profits after the costs of the mailer itself had been accounted for. So the way to compare the two mailers correctly is to compare the contribution from each mailer. The contribution from the letter was an average of $.29 per piece mailed. The contribution from the VHS package was $1.14 per piece mailed. Both sides of the test were profitable, but the side with the video tape was much more profitable.

Obviously the VHS package was well worth the extra investment, so we mailed all of our future packages with VHS tapes. This became our new "standard" or "control" direct-mail package.

Split Test Number Two

Our next split test with this direct-mail campaign was to simply try a different name on the video. We created a split test with two packages that had the exact same offer, but one video had the same name we used on our original offer. It said, "New Customer Offer." The other one said, "Student Pilot Offer." The contribution was $.84 for the new customer offer and $2.14 for the student pilot offer. We had another obvious winner. What we decided from this was that how you address people matters, and you should pay attention when they express their preference. The folks we were mailing to apparently thought of themselves as "student pilots," not "new customers," and responded accordingly.

The Numeric Difference from Our First Split Test

It's important to note that our original test showed a contribution from our VHS package offer of $1.14, and this new test showed the exact same offer to this group with a contribution margin of $.84. You might think that the exact same offer should always yield the same result, but that's not true. Technically, it wasn't the *exact* same offer because it was sent to a different list on a different date. The difference in numbers may have been because we mailed to a different list, or it may have been different because of some slight change in the economy or national news. It may have been because of something a competitor released to the marketplace. It may have been the time of year ("seasonal variation"). The point here is that you can only compare two sets of numbers in a controlled, scientific split if *everything* is the same except the one factor you're testing. Our only takeaway in this second test is that the name "student pilot" continued to be much more effective.

Another Name Split Test, this Time with a Deadline

For our next test we broke the rules a little bit. The goal was to test two names, but we also added a deadline. The deadline was the same for both offers, so testing the names against each other was the only true measurable difference. However, we probably should have done a different split test for the deadline using the same name. The result of this test was that the Student Pilot Summer Special had a contribution margin of $1.87 and the New Pilot Special's contribution margin was $1.10. The "Student Pilot" name was the clear winner.

Printing Cost Savings Test Turned into an Even Bigger Profit

We were creating these mailer packets with several printed pieces days or weeks in advance of receiving each list from the FAA. Because we never knew how many names we would get from the FAA, we always printed hundreds more dated letters and dated offer descriptions than we needed. If we received 1,500 names and had 2,000 pieces printed, we had to throw away 500 extras.

In order to try to better control our printing costs, we created our entire packet with the letters, brochures, VHS tapes, and more with no date, then we simply inserted an orange card with the offer deadline information on it. Our letter and even our video contained language that said, "See the orange card for dates and important details." Then we mailed a split test with 50 percent of the recipients getting the originally structured offer with a dated letter, and the other group receiving the offer where the only date information was on that orange card. Our hope was that we would at least get similar results so we could spend less on printing and stop throwing away so many dated extra letters. But the results were even better than we had hoped—the orange card version generated significantly better results. The contribution margins were $1.51 for the dated letter and $2.65 for the orange-card version. Saving money on printing while getting better sales results was a win-win!

When you analyze the performance of these offers, you might think that the reason the dated orange card performed better is because the orange card itself captured attention. That may be the case, but scientifically we don't know. The good news is that it doesn't matter. We just knew the results were better and that this could become our new baseline standard. In other words, our new control package.

The VHS Video Sleeve

After some discussions about what we might test next (we thought about card colors, other course name changes, other pamphlets), we decided to put a printed sleeve (cardboard case) around the VHS tape in the package. These printed sleeves cost us fifteen cents each and we printed a bit of detailed information about what was on the tape itself. The sleeve said, "Play this video right now and in just 26 minutes you will learn how to make flawless crosswind landings and how you could win a free airplane."

You've probably guessed that the printed sleeve did better—which it did—but it's actually quite surprising how *much* better it did. The offer with no VHS sleeve yielded a contribution margin of $2.72 per piece mailed, while the offer with the sleeve netted $5.25. We were mailing around 10,000 mailers a month. At an average increase in the profit per mailer of $2.53, we were now making an extra $25,300 per month. And that increased profit kept coming month after month. This is what makes it fun to be an entrepreneur!

Personalization

Something we know from our sales experience is that addressing someone in person by their name improves the connection and helps a person feel recognized and valued. We always address people by name in conversations, so it was only natural that we would consider testing to see if including a person's name on our letters would yield better results.

It Tanked!

In this case, we tested the package with the sleeve against the same package that included the recipient's name. The package with the sleeve did as well as it did before, but the package that included the recipient's name in the letter did not even pay for the cost of the mailing. It lost money.

Personalized communications with existing customers is almost always very well received, but in this case we were working from that FAA list and people may have felt as if we were somehow invading their privacy or being too pushy. Again, the "why" doesn't matter. We just knew it was not something we would do again with prospects.

Video Quality

In the days when we were mass-producing our own VHS tapes, those duplication machines were especially expensive equipment. When our team suggested upgrading that equipment so the marketing videos would be better quality, we wanted to make sure that the improved quality of the videos would be a worthwhile investment. That meant we should conduct a new split test to see if there was any effect.

We tracked the responses from people who received the marketing tapes created on the more expensive duplication machines (as opposed to the old technology with lower-quality videos), and we found that the old tapes had a contribution margin of $2.08, while the newer, higher-quality tapes yielded $3.27 per unit. We upgraded.

Card Color

We don't generally test "whispers" during our split tests. Anything that is a small difference (a little graphic, font choice, etc.) is rarely worth split-testing because those smaller elements don't generally get big results. The color of our offer card wasn't something we thought too hard about, but since we had already done so many bigger split tests, we tried a card-color test and it turned out the contribution margin of blue cards was $1.29 and green cards was $1.80.

Is It Worthwhile to Work around Slow Mail/Shipping?

One of our competitors was shipping packages first class, so their materials were getting to customers much more quickly than our third-class mail packages. They weren't sending the big VHS packs with support letters and brochures like we were, so their costs were more manageable. First class for our VHS package was far too expensive, so we thought we might send a first-class postcard in advance of the offer to let prospects know that the big package was on the way. In this particular test, we were putting out a good offer at a good time of year. The offer with the postcard sent in advance yielded a contribution margin of $3.24, while the exact same package with no postcard in advance had a contribution margin of $6.80—more than twice the response with no postcard. Not sending out the postcard was an easy decision.

More Ways to Save on Shipping

So far, we had been sending materials in bulky padded envelopes, and we felt those bulky envelopes garnered more attention from customers. Then we looked at shipping everything in a neater box because it was cheaper to buy and prepare for mailing, and even the postage was lower. In that split test, we found that the contribution margin was $4.12 for our original padded envelope, while the neater, cheaper box got us $7.20 per unit. Now the box was our new baseline, control-package standard.

This example was based on direct mail and obvious physical differences, but split-testing is just as much a part of our marketing when we place digital offers online, buy ads on YouTube, or put ads in the few industry magazines still being published. In fact, split-testing and tracking is even easier with all the digital marketing tools available these days.

THE ONLY TIME YOU SHOULDN'T BOTHER SPLIT-TESTING A DIRECT-RESPONSE MARKETING EFFORT

Split-testing is scientific. If we had never done any split-testing and had only sent out the same original letter we started with, we would have probably continued getting a contribution margin around $.29 per unit, instead of more than $7 per unit. Since we were mailing about 10,000 mailers per month, that increase in bottom line per month of $6.31 per mailer yielded an increase in profit of $67,100 per month, month in and out.

Obviously, it took time and money to discover what worked best in our efforts. We avoided testing "whispers." We kept testing big ideas. We never sent out a direct-response marketing piece without split-testing.

The only time you shouldn't split-test is when your target audience is too small. You should only test when you expect at least fifty responses per side. If for some reason we received a group of just a few hundred names from the FAA, we would either wait until we had more names and split that list 50/50 with the next big batch of names, or we would just send the un-split single offer that we had tested and proven to be the most effective by then to the small list.

If you do have a big-enough target audience, not split-testing major offer differences with each direct-response marketing spend is wasting money.

HOW TO GET FREE PUBLICITY

Publishers Frequently Pick up Press Releases and Run Them for Free

The key to getting free publicity is to write a press release that the publisher can pick up and run without editing. You should assume all editors are overworked, and you should try to make their job of dealing with your news as easy as possible.

Focus on the Interests of the Reader—the Star of the Show

Press releases are more likely to be picked up if the release addresses the ultimate reader and talks about the benefits to the reader from the product or event discussed in the release. As an example, you could say, "Pilots can now take a free video course, "Understanding Aircraft

Marshalling Signals," from King Schools to help them quickly learn the signals used by aircraft marshallers at a busy ramp." (An aircraft marshaller is a person on the tarmac who uses handheld batons to direct pilots regarding taxiing and approaching the proper gate or parking place.) This is much more appealing to an editor and much more likely to get the release published than leading the press release with "King Schools announces …." Starting off talking about King Schools instead of the reader will likely appear to the publisher too much like free advertising.

One appeal that works well is to tie your press release or event into a charity, if you can. Doing a promotion or sponsoring a program that also promotes or benefits a charity, especially a local one, is a good way to get extra attention from newspapers. Most of them have a strong public-service orientation.

Write as If You Were a Journalist Writing for a Local Newspaper

Continue writing to that reader throughout the press release in an interesting journalistic (not advertising) style that a publication can print or publish without re-editing.

Your release should be about 100–150 words and consist of the release itself, a cover letter, and a good action photo or graphic. Don't forget to include your company name and address early in the news release so people will know how to reach you. These days most businesses would usually send that content by email.

Use Language Your Reader Will Understand

Be careful with abbreviations and jargon that might not be understood, particularly by a reader new to your product or service. Construct your news release as if you were having a conversation with a member of your target audience. What would you like to tell them first, and how would you say it? Write that "conversation"—really, it *is* that simple.

Use Quotes to Add Emotional Content

Add quotes—they are pictures painted with words. Quotes allow you to praise your product or event in a way that an editor never would. They also allow you to add personal perspective and human interest. Anytime you feel you want to say something starting with "You," make it a quote—from someone in the company, from a customer, etc.

Don't get fancy. When inserting quotes in a story, you don't have to agonize over ten different ways to say, "He said." That'll do just fine, actually.

Use Who, What, When, Where, Why

Keep in mind the famous five "Ws" when writing your release: who, what, when, where, and why. Those five Ws give your reader and the editor the information they need to make sense of your story.

Keep it simple and on message. If you have more than one message, write more than one release.

Use Images and Captions, Headlines and Subheads

Send pictures that are relevant to the story. That includes clip art, logos, and digital snapshots. Include suggested captions and use them to tell a story. Captions are among the first and most frequently read part of a story. Captions should not just describe a photo but should also tell the story of the photo. Headlines and subheads are also a great place to tell your story.

Get to the Point and Tell Your Story Early

When an editor needs to shorten a press release to make it fit the available space, the easiest way to do that is to just chop off paragraphs at the end of the release. The editor assumes that all the important information is early in the release—so you should make sure it is.

TV and Radio Stations Are Hungry for News Too

Television and radio stations need to fill many hours per day with information for their viewers or listeners. If you want to make a guest appearance on TV or radio to talk about your product or service, call or email the personality on the show or the program director. If you have a news item, contact the news desk.

The whole idea is to be interesting, so you should clearly indicate what is unusual or novel about what you have to say. If you do get an interview, you'll want to be prepared. One big help to the interviewer is to prepare a list of possible questions that the interviewer can ask you. After all, you know more about your product, service, or event than they possibly could! Of course, you will want to have good answers prepared for those questions.

It would be nice to have some idea of how many people saw or heard you and liked what you had to say. One way to find out is to offer something of perceived value—this will give you a chance to get your name and address out. A great item would be a checklist or document they could download from your website, because that gives you a chance to capture their contact information.

So When Should You Use Press Releases?

You should use press releases at every possible opportunity: when you have new products or services you want folks to know about, when you hire or promote someone, when you have some community involvement, or whenever you have an event that might be in any way newsworthy. Constantly be thinking, "How can this event be used for publicity or made into news?" As you read the newspaper, think about how your product or service can tie into current events. Can you show a tie-in to a holiday or special week or day? Or to a community event taking place?

Remember, They Need You

Don't be reluctant to submit press releases. They are an important part of the community and give publishers something to work with. Publications are hungry for your news. They have space they need to fill! About 50 percent of the articles you see in a newspaper every day come from press releases or publicity campaigns. Make sure you get your share of free publicity.

CHAPTER

11

CREATING AN OUTSTANDING CUSTOMER EXPERIENCE

You can, as an entrepreneur, make one particular investment that will continue to improve your bottom line for the rest of your business life. We're talking about investing in providing a fantastic customer experience.

Before we get too far along, we need to define outstanding customer experience. We used to refer to outstanding "customer service," but over time we began to feel that the word "service" was limiting. "Service" seems to cast the expression into terms of one person doing work for another. Our more recent way of describing what we are looking for is to provide an outstanding "experience"—the idea being to immerse the customer in satisfaction.

Some people say the way to define what we are looking for is an experience that exceeds the customer's expectations. In other words, it is a customer experience so good, the customer didn't even see it coming.

We had that happen to us when we arrived at a hotel in Mexico called Las Hadas to check in, and there was no front desk. The staff simply asked us to sit down in the lobby, gave everyone in our party a glass of nice wine, sat down beside us, and conducted the registration.

Then there is a hotel on Ambergris Cay in the Turks and Caicos that also gave us a seat and wine, but they completely dispensed with the check-in process because they knew who was coming. They assigned us a golf cart and a butler who gave us a dedicated cell phone to call him. He stood by for our every command, including hot food served in the room. In each of these cases, we did not see the experience coming. It certainly exceeded our expectations.

In every business, careful thought will help you come up with a way you could provide an unexpectedly outstanding experience for your customers. Such things can be expensive to do and the decisions have to be made in the context of having to make a profit. It all depends on the clientele you wish to appeal to.

The few businesses with a true focus on an outstanding customer experience get incredibly powerful word-of-mouth advertising you couldn't pay for if you wanted to. And that's just one of many benefits of providing an outstanding customer experience.

STANDARD CUSTOMER SERVICE IS POINTLESS

If you've been to a restaurant, a big box store, a grocery store, or a gas station in the past week, you've probably had a bad customer experience. It happens so often you might not even realize it.

Maybe you had to use self-checkout because all the lines with a cashier were far too long. Maybe you waited in a five-minute line at a "convenience" store to pay for your gas because the two people in front of you had a hard time picking out all the lottery scratch-off ticket options they wanted. Maybe you walked into a sit-down chain restaurant that doesn't take reservations, and you got ignored for three or four minutes while the staffers at the host podium discussed wait-staff table assignments. You finally got the attention of one who eventually made eye contact with you, only to hear them utter the single syllable, "Yeah?" Then once you got your name added to the list, they handed you a pager and said, "It's gonna be twenty to thirty minutes. Make sure your whole party is with you when this buzzes to let you know your table is ready."

You are paying for groceries or gasoline or dinner out and you're being treated in a way that requires the lowest possible level of customer interaction. You're practically being dismissed as an inconvenience to those working at the store or restaurant. Yet they need your money to stay in business. They don't intend it as an insult to you, but still, you are the one having the bad experience.

Another great example of a terrible customer experience is when a company or a medical office runs you through an extensive phone menu when you are trying to reach someone. These phone trees require people to listen to a list of options, and if they struggle through the process long enough, they might actually get to a live human being so they can explain their issue and get a little guidance. Unfortunately, a lot of those calls still get directed to someone's voicemail.

This low-quality customer experience is now a "standard" we have all just come to expect. In the modern economy, this seems to be a growing trend. A poor customer experience is so prevalent, we have all just started to expect it. Ironically, that's good news—because it's easy to be better.

WHEN THE BAR IS SET LOW IT'S EASY TO BE GOOD, BUT GOOD STILL ISN'T GOOD ENOUGH

Just because most (or maybe all) of your competitors are delivering a standard, unremarkable customer experience, that does not mean that being a little better will make you stand out. Sure, it would be easy to deliver your products and/or experience while slightly exceeding poor customer-experience standards already in place, but it is not that difficult to figure out how to deliver an outstanding customer experience.

Think about it this way: If weak customer experience is what we generally expect and we go somewhere that's a little bit better, we might be a little happier. There's no lasting impression that causes behavior changes in your buying patterns.

What can you do to be better? You can start by learning about what the customer experience is in your industry. Be sure to keep in mind that learning about your industry's standard customer experience should be done *only* to give you a starting point for reference. Ultimately, your goal should be to deliver much more than the standard. You need to get past good and shoot for *great*. You should deliver a *fantastic* customer experience!

TESTIMONIALS ARE GOOD

Happy customers are a good thing and they lead smart entrepreneurs to consider capturing a testimonial for marketing purposes. Testimonials play a role in the decision-making process for many potential customers, so you should make an effort to collect them and use them as a part of your marketing.

When someone is considering buying a product or hiring someone to do a service, they look for indicators that they are selecting a trustworthy company or a quality product or service. We all read reviews, if they're available, especially for higher-ticket items. Hearing from a customer who paid for that product or service and then commented about how they liked it helps customers feel more comfortable spending their own money on that same product or service. It's frequently recognized that busy restaurants tend to attract more customers, and restaurants with just two or three cars in the parking lot tend to discourage customers and can have a tough time staying in business.

You should do what you can to collect positive comments about your own offerings so you can post them on your website and include them in printed ads, emails, videos, etc. And while it's obvious that no business would publish bad comments about themselves, testimonials have a major impact in your marketing because they are the words of a customer and not the business owner. This kind of evidence of a good customer experience is powerful marketing.

THE ULTIMATE TESTIMONIAL

World-renowned business book author Ken Blanchard has described the benefits of delivering a fantastic customer experience. He calls extremely happy customers "raving fans" in his book of the same name.[2]

The point of his book is to suggest that you create customers who are so impressed with the amazing customer experience you provide that they become active, outspoken, word-of-mouth advertisers for your business—that they are simply so thrilled with the customer experience you have created for them, they feel compelled to tell others about how fantastic their experience was. And fantastic testimonials will frequently make sales for you that you never expected.

Beyond word-of-mouth from a customer to other potential customers, there's yet another benefit: repeat customers.

If you delivered a customer-service experience on par with or slightly better than others in your industry, then when it comes time for a former customer to select a place where they will be spending money on a new purchase, you might get the business—but your competition could just as well get the business instead. If your competition's location is closer, or their business name or web address is easier to remember, your slightly better customer experience won't be enough to compel them to make any extra effort to do business with you again.

On the other hand, if you have delivered a remarkable customer experience that is memorable and well beyond that of your competition, the happiness your customer experienced the last time they did business with you will compel them to seek you out again. Even if it means spending a little more time or money to make that happen. A

---

[2] Ken Blanchard and Sheldon Bowles, *Raving Fans: A Revolutionary Approach to Customer Service* (New York City: William Morrow, 1993).

great restaurant with wonderful service is worth a drive. An online auto parts store that had a specialist spend time on the phone with a customer to find an unusual part, or maybe emailed them a link to a video that showed exactly how to install that part, will get repeat customers.

A fantastic customer experience will generate both new customers and repeat customers.

THE RITZ-CARLTON STANDARD

As you can imagine, with all the flying we do in our business and all the places we go, we have stayed in countless hotels. Customer service is quite similar with most hotels, but one hotel chain stands out well above the rest: The Ritz-Carlton. The luxury circumstances are nice, but some other hotels have similar offerings. The real stand-out aspect of The Ritz-Carlton properties is the training of their staff.

Specifically, Ritz-Carlton staff is great because of how employees are trained to engage with guests. For instance, one time while we were in line approaching the front desk and waiting to check in, we could see that all the front-desk staffers were busily checking in the guests who were in line ahead of us. During our wait, another Ritz-Carlton employee carrying a clipboard approached the front desk from across the room. It was obvious he was on a mission of some sort and needed to talk with one of the associates checking in other guests, but instead of just walking straight to an employee with his head down while ignoring those of us checking in, he paused on his way. He intentionally stepped toward those of us waiting in line and started talking with us.

"I'm sorry you have to wait to check in, but our staff is working as fast as they can," he said. Then he added with a smile, "And I'm really sorry I can't get behind the counter and speed up the check-in process, but I don't know how to work those computers." Everybody in line smiled and most of us laughed a little bit at his slightly funny comment. Then he engaged in a bit of small talk with us and others in line about where we were from and how long we'd be staying with them. As he wrapped up that light conversation with the group, including answering some questions about the hotel and the local area, he continued walking to the front desk with his clipboard and briefly asked one of the front-desk staff a question. That staffer looked something up quickly on the computer and the first employee jotted something on his clipboard. As he walked away, he said goodbye to us, his new friends, who were still waiting in line to check in.

Consider what happened over the period of just a minute or two. A Ritz-Carlton employee saw a group of people standing in line, waiting to check in. He needed to exchange some information with an employee at the front desk who was already busy serving customers as they checked in for their stay. In practically any other hotel, you would expect that person to completely ignore those of us standing in line so he wouldn't have to address possible concerns about the slow check-in process or the time spent in line. This gentleman defused that entire situation before it had a chance to occur. He did that by recognizing and valuing a group of customers waiting in line. He engaged with us in a completely friendly manner.

By making eye contact and conversing with customers directly instead of ignoring us, he caused us to automatically like him. Then when he bypassed us and went up to the front desk to speak with an employee who was checking guests in, we had no problem at all with his action. If he had silently walked past all of us, ignored us, and then effectively jumped the line to talk with a fellow employee (and slow down the check-in process), we would all probably have been silently a little bit annoyed with him. Instead, he was our new friend. We had no problem with his speaking with the front-desk employee. He had demonstrated that he valued us.

After spending several days at this wonderful Ritz-Carlton resort, we realized we had enjoyed conversations with quite a few employees. Of course, because of our interest in customer experience, we asked some of those employees about Ritz-Carlton customer-experience policies and training. We came to discover that all employees at The Ritz-Carlton are taught to make eye contact and some sort of verbal connection with any guest. They use a "10 and 5" rule: anytime they are within ten feet of any guest, they should make eye contact and smile. When they are within five feet of any guest, they should smile and say, "Hello," as long as they aren't interrupting.

We felt valued as guests at The Ritz-Carlton and our interaction with countless employees was largely responsible for that experience.

Customer experience is always first class when everyone pays attention. You never feel overlooked. You always feel appreciated.

Additionally, when someone asks a Ritz-Carlton employee for directions to somewhere in the hotel, the employee is not allowed to just give directions—they are required to escort the guest to that location. And if a guest complains about something outside an employee's normal work area, such as a housekeeping issue to the manager of the gift shop, the Ritz-Carlton employee hearing the complaint must take ownership of it and commit to resolving it. They are not allowed to suggest that you call housekeeping—they are required to handle it themselves. These are wonderful examples of greatly exceeding expectations.

THE KING SCHOOLS APPROACH TO CUSTOMER EXPERIENCE

At King Schools, we have worked to develop tools and guidelines that help all our employees deliver a wonderful customer experience. Below we've listed our three principles for an outstanding customer experience:

1. *Get the job done.*

This makes sense in any business at every level, but it still sits in first place when we describe our three principles for outstanding customer experience. Sometimes you have to state the obvious. We aren't reciting some feel-good agenda that starts with something like, "Try your best." We have smart, capable employees whom we trust, and we fully expect them to do what they need to do in order for their work to be fully accomplished.

2. *Be available.*

Our core values are to solicit feedback from our customers and be very responsive to it. For nearly fifty years, every course we have delivered has had a provision for feedback. In the early days, it was a self-reply postcard that the customer filled out. These days customers are asked for electronic feedback at the completion of every course. We also have email, phones, and live chat to deal with ad-hoc issues. We credit our core value of being responsive to customer feedback as having been instrumental in helping us keep our courses in line with customer needs.

3. Over-communicate.

When a customer does express a concern, it is our responsibility to listen to the concern, make sure we understand it, and be thoroughly responsive to it.

AN OVER-COMMUNICATION SUCCESS STORY

A contractor in Central Florida found himself frustrated by a client who constantly called him on his cell about a remodel project. The contractor had a great reputation in the marketplace and had many happy customers for both remodels and new home construction. However, this particular customer was frustrated with the dates and delivery times for each of the steps of the remodel.

In the construction business, it is very common to predict an overall budget along with an overall completion date. But it would be extremely unusual for every single phase of a construction project to happen exactly as projected without adjustments. For instance, kitchen cabinets might be installed a couple of days late. Windows planned for replacement might be delayed because the hardware vendor shipped an incorrect part. The electrician who was slated to install new ceiling lights on Wednesday might have been delayed in finishing a job at a different location and needed to reschedule. Everything from weather to staffing to paperwork mix-ups can slow things down a little, and practically every contractor uses subcontractors who have their own production speed bumps.

Most contractors who have been in the business for a few years calculate the big-picture time and budget estimates correctly, but only a genuine psychic could project every little hiccup. Unfortunately for contractors, very few clients who aren't in the residential-building field themselves understand these mid-project delays.

While the contractor was on site at various locations with current projects, he would receive several phone calls from this one anxious client. He got to the point where he would let the calls go to voicemail and then return them at the end of the day. The contractor dreaded those calls because he felt like he was always having to reassure his client. He had to stop what he was doing and focus on their project in the middle of managing a dozen other projects.

Then the contractor changed his approach. One afternoon while visiting this client's property, he decided to do an informal "walk through" video with his cell phone. In that video, he explained what was going on at the house and pointed out that incorrect handles were sent for the kitchen cabinetry. He pointed out how this would slow things down a bit, so they would work on the bedroom closet doors while they waited for correct parts. Then by the middle of the following week, the correct hardware would be on site and those handles would be corrected. He walked around inside the property and showed progress on wall painting and door installations and other positive developments. He uploaded this forty-five-second summary-style video as a private file on YouTube and texted a link to the client.

Everything changed! The client couldn't get over how happy they were with the detailed overview of the progress taking place at their property and the personal video explanation from the lead contractor himself. The video showed actual progress and allowed the contractor to preemptively inform the client about any little slowdowns and how they were being addressed. The client stopped making regular daily calls and just periodically sent text messages to let the contractor know how happy they were with each video update. That client became a raving fan!

IN-HOUSE OVER-COMMUNICATION

Interestingly, when the pandemic of 2020 happened and King Schools staffers all started working from home, these same three principles for creating an outstanding customer experience—get your work done, be available, over-communicate—gained a new level of importance.

These principles helped us remind ourselves what is most important. Because we no longer had the luxury of popping by a co-worker's office to get clarification on something, we found it especially valuable to emphasize the importance of being available to one another (and customers, of course) in every way possible. Even if you don't love receiving email (or text or phone calls or Zoom meetings—everybody has a communication style they don't love), the new working-from-home demands meant that we all had to pay extra attention to all communications channels.

THE GOOD NEWS FOR YOU

Many local businesses are allowing the customer experience to drop in quality. Because your competition is not as good as it used to be, it's easier to be outstanding.

Online there are pop-up "chat" windows that offer help or guidance to resolve customer experience issues. The good ones are staffed by an actual human, but even then, in most cases, those people are handling four or five or ten customer chats at the same time. Those staffers often copy and paste answers to common questions, and their cookie-cutter replies are slow since they are helping several people at once. (Talk about multitasking!) The really frustrating chat help options are run using artificial intelligence (AI) programs. As good as many AI interfaces have become in recent years, they still make mistakes. They just aren't as smart or capable as a human having a quick Q&A with a customer to understand the issue and provide the best response.

If you want raving fans for customers, your path is clear. You must make it as easy as possible for your customers to connect with a human quickly, using the communications channel of their choice (phone, email, chat, etc.), and to get a response that addresses their question or solves their problem. Respond quickly! That means fast responses to both concerns and compliments.

THE HUMAN SIDE OF TECHNOLOGY

There is no question that technology is a fantastic benefit to modern society. In most of the world, each person has a device in their pocket that allows them to connect with others, receive direct communications, play games, listen to music, and connect to the internet for countless additional capabilities. It's truly amazing! And as we have emphasized, technology can be leveraged to manage direct marketing, split-testing, and of course, delivery of products and services. But there's an important consideration:

"The purpose of technology is to help us be more human."

— John King

Smart entrepreneurs use technology to connect better with their customers, suppliers, and fellow employees. They don't use it to distance themselves from customers and provide automated customer service. The human connection is what really matters. Technology gives us more avenues to connect, and it gives us the ability to make that connection more quickly.

A QUICK TEST

Once your company is big enough that there are people answering customer calls, you should call your company to see what the customer experience is like. "Secret shoppers" aren't just for retail stores. If your staff would recognize your voice, get a friend to call your company on speaker while you listen in and see how things go.

THE SILENT SCREAM

We share the belief that Ken Blanchard expressed in his book *Raving Fans*. There are three kinds of customers, he says:

1. The silent customer

2. The angry, complaining customer
3. The raving fan

Silent customers are definitely not raving fans, and they aren't going to be loyal repeat customers if there are any other options available to them from your competitors. If you're lucky, those silent customers are satisfied or even a little happy. However, it's much more likely that they are disappointed.

It may seem like quite a leap in logical thinking to suggest that the majority of silent customers are unhappy, but think about it this way: If someone is very disappointed and think they're being charged for a car repair that didn't work, or a meal that was served cold and tasted terrible, they might get angry enough and verbal enough to complain and ask for their money back.

It's also possible that a customer may be a longtime patron and they could take a minute to tell you that they normally have a great experience with you, but their latest purchase was sub-par, so you know and you have a chance to fix it. They know your standards are better than what happened just now and they feel like you will care enough to improve.

But when a meal was unremarkable and the service was slow, if the hostess asks you on your way out the door, "How was everything?" most people just say "fine" and keep walking. That's it. They have no connection to the business that makes them believe there may be value in sharing their bad experience with the hostess. And they feel like they don't owe you anything—it just doesn't matter. People who say "everything was fine" probably aren't very happy even if nothing especially bad happened. They're just barely satisfied and won't be motivated to make any effort to become a repeat customer. Silent customers are not happy customers. The goal should always be to have raving fans.

Alternatively, if someone is blown away by the quality of what you have delivered, along with the great interaction with staff (think Ritz-Carlton), then you'll hear from that raving fan. They just won't be able to help themselves!

RAVING FANS AREN'T JUST CUSTOMERS

When your business is structured correctly and your staff is empowered and encouraged to cultivate raving fans, that corporate culture has an energy that resonates throughout the company. That means your suppliers will be excited to work with you. Your employees will like their managers and the people who work for them. The raving-fan attitude will be a noteworthy part of your company, and everybody who comes in contact with your business will know it because they'll feel it and be an active participant.

At King Schools, we consider everyone who comes in contact with our products and services to be potential raving fans. When we design a course for Cessna, we don't just have to make the students happy. We want every person from Cessna who reviews our course content to interact with our staff in the style of that Ritz-Carlton experience. We want every single touchpoint between King Schools and Cessna to be a great experience worthy of positive comments. We want them *all* to be raving fans.

When we interact with the company that prints our catalog, our designers go out of their way to make sure the printer has everything needed, on time, and in the correct format. We pay very promptly for our printing, so our jobs always get priority handling. We do everything we can to be a good customer and we get great service as a result. In fact, during the COVID-19 pandemic, when our printer was having to "fire" customers due to shortages of paper, ink, employees and available press time, they reassured us that we were a desirable customer and they did not foresee ever not wanting, or being able, to print our catalog. Our suppliers love working with us and we want them to be raving fans.

We intend for our clients, employees, and suppliers to all be our raving fans.

OUR STARTING POINTS

There are a handful of specific things we use to set up our employees for success when it comes to their role in creating raving fans. You'll recognize these from our chapter on non-manipulative selling and our discussions about hiring good employees, because the very same tools that help you sell ethically and that create a quality work environment are the same tools that empower employees in every single interaction with clients, prospects, suppliers, vendors, and co-workers:

- Know your purpose
- Know your values
- Know the company mission statement
- Know your USP (Unique Selling Proposition)

EMPOWER STAFF TO ENGAGE

Think again of the Ritz-Carlton experience with respect to interaction between customers and staff—their approach was to have every staffer interact with clients. This includes top-level management, maintenance staff, kitchen staff, and housekeeping staff. Everyone.

At King Schools, every employee who interacts with anyone as a part of their work is encouraged to be engaging and happy. They should be friendly and conversational. They should always give off positive energy and convey that they are there to help. There are companies that guide their employees to all "'stay in their lane" and only engage others, especially customers, if it is necessary to complete their job. For us, positive customer interactions are a necessary part of *everyone's* job description.

Beyond the core principles of get the job done, be available, over-communicate, know your purpose, know your values, know the company mission statement, and know the company's USP, King Schools employees are encouraged to ask questions and listen to the customer. This is encouraged across the board, not just for salespeople. Consider that the first Ritz-Carlton employee who spoke with those of us waiting in line was not specifically on a mission to sell something to us. He wasn't doing customer research. He was simply being engaging with clients to make them raving fans.

BE FLEXIBLE AND LISTEN WELL—JOHN'S STORY

In my teen years at King's One Stop, it was my job to always wash customers' car windows while filling up cars that stopped in for gas. I was taught that people appreciated that free extra effort and I should always do it.

We had a regular customer who would zip in some mornings and quickly prepay by handing me a dollar or two, not enough to fill his tank, and he'd say something like, "Just give me a dollar's worth." This was different, because most people would get a fill-up, pay, and then get change back. Not this guy. And when I would start washing his windshield, he'd say, "I don't need that. The windshield is fine." This happened a few times, and I never really caught on that I should always skip the windshield with this guy when he would pull in fast and pre-pay. I just did what I was taught and never adjusted to this customer's different style.

Looking back, I think he was probably late for work and just wanted some gas to get him where he was going. He wanted it fast and he didn't want the extra service of the windshield cleaning or the hassle of waiting for change. He would have been a happier customer if I had been flexible and listened to what he really wanted.

Ritz-Carlton has the ten-foot rule for employees to engage in a friendly, upbeat manner with every customer, but they don't have a specific script for employees to follow. That would create "robot" employees. Ritz-Carlton employees not only have the flexibility to talk about any number of things, they also have the flexibility to smile and say, "Hello," and then say absolutely nothing else—and even go right back to what they were doing if the customer seems busy or seems like they just don't want to talk. Employees should talk to customers as long as those customers seem like they are open to talking.

FIXING PROBLEMS—THE ONLY TWO ROLES THAT CAN BE PLAYED WHEN THERE IS A COMPLAINT

This approach is based on the concept that there are only two roles that can be played when there is a complaint.

The roles are:

- "That's outrageous!"
- "It's no big deal."

When one role is chosen, social convention automatically assigns the opposite role to the other party.

For instance, let's assume a customer is complaining that we sent them the wrong course. One approach would be for the person who is receiving the complaint to say, "What, we shipped the wrong course? I am so sorry. You shouldn't have to put up with that. That's outrageous! That really disrupts your schedule. I'm sorry we did that to you. We'll make it right. What would you like me to do?"

One of the keys to the success of this approach is that the King Schools staffer receiving the complaint immediately and automatically accepts blame for the customer not receiving what they wanted—we do that even if we suspect it was the customer's fault and not ours. It moves the conversation away from whose fault it was to what remedy would work best.

This approach automatically assigns the other party the "it's no big deal" role.

So the other party will say something like, "Well actually, it's no problem. I was rushing too fast. It gave me an opportunity to slow my schedule down and take more time studying for the exam."

On the other hand, let's assume the King Schools staffer receiving the complaint broke with our policy and said something like, "Why would we ship the wrong course? Are you sure you didn't order the wrong course? Can't you change your schedule to allow time for the replacement course to arrive?"

This "no big deal" response on our part almost guarantees the "it's outrageous" response from the customer: "I know what I ordered! I shouldn't have to reschedule. I have the time set aside for the course and test and you guys really messed up my schedule."

This concept sounds so simple that it can seem like an exaggeration or over-simplification when we tell employees about it, but it absolutely works, and it really is this simple. Some employees do require some coaching to get their minds wrapped around the concept of accepting the blame. They have to be coached past the mindset of never admitting the company is wrong, especially when it's not.

You should try this technique sometime. When you see it work, it is almost miraculous.

Our concept, which seems like an exaggeration, is that if the employee receiving the complaint plays the "it's outrageous" role and accepts the blame whether it was our fault or not, the complaining customer will feel compelled to calmly de-escalate the interaction. In a customer/employee interaction, if one person says, "THAT'S OUTRAGEOUS!!," the other person has no choice but to respond with "It's not that bad—it's really no big deal" to de-escalate it.

Even if your employee uses some other wording to describe their reaction, the concept holds true that they should play the "it's outrageous" role and accept the blame in the interaction. That doesn't mean respond louder. That doesn't mean they need to swear back if the customer used swear words to launch their complaint. They just need to convincingly play that role. If it fits their personality better, they might say, "I can't believe that happened to you. Let's get to the bottom of this right away!" Or "That's ridiculous. I need to fix this right now!" These strong customer-advocate positions always get the customer to scale down the intensity from their original complaint and take the position that "it's not a big deal."

"I am NOT Patient"

By the way, one sentence we would like to stamp out from the world is, "Thank you for your patience." Why?

- Use of the expression implies to the customer that you are providing a customer experience that requires patience.

- It implies that the customer would be impatient unless you told them not to be. (The expression tends to make us impatient when we hear it, even if we weren't before.)

- You should never assume you know what a customer is feeling. They may not be patient at all…and that is perfectly OK.

- If time has gone by, it is *much better* to *apologize for the delay* than to assume they were patient during that time, and imply that we *expect* them to be patient.

CREATING RAVING FANS WILL PAY OFF IN WAYS YOU NEVER IMAGINED

You'll sell more. Customers will advertise for you word-of-mouth style. You'll develop loyal, repeat customers. When there is a problem, those loyal customers will care enough to let you know. You'll have happy suppliers and you'll have happy employees. A fantastic customer experience that delivers well beyond industry-standard customer service is a mission-critical investment that will always pay off.

CHAPTER

12

OUR "HARD-AND-FAST RULES FOR SUCCESS"

You have what it takes to be a successful entrepreneur, so now it is time to take the next step on your journey. To make your entrepreneurial success a reality, continue practicing PLAY–TNT and collecting valuable Scrabble letters. Continue researching your marketplace, marketing efforts, your business model, and your product or service offerings, and stay open to growth and change.

This book was developed to be an evergreen resource to help entrepreneurs at every stage along their business development path. As you put into practice the tools and ideas presented in these pages, you will undoubtedly improve the success of your business, and you should make it a point to revisit this book again in a year or a couple of months. Come back any time you run into a business challenge and you'll discover (or rediscover) tools, processes, and mindsets to help you continue your success journey.

You already know this: entrepreneurship is a gift. If you've read this far, you know that the gift is to everyone involved in the process, from the customers to the vendors and suppliers and, of course, the entrepreneurs themselves. Beyond that, entrepreneurship is a gift to your local community because you pay taxes, and the community is further supported by all the places your employees go for dinner or groceries, send their kids to schools, and even donate to charities of all kinds.

There's a positive ripple effect that all starts when an entrepreneur decides they want to deliver goods or services to someone who needs them, and who is able to pay an amount that generates a profit.

Throughout this book, we have attempted to provide insights to best practices, tools, structures, and thought processes to help you master your own entrepreneurial venture and hopefully smooth your path to success by shortening the learning curve.

As we conclude our overview and you embark (or continue) on your entrepreneurial journey, we suggest the following tools and concepts that you can use as a quick reference guide:

GETTING AHEAD

- It should be a goal to leave everyone who comes in contact with you better off.
- The way to get other people to do what you want is to use the dynamite tool of TNT:
  - o Trustworthiness is established
  - o Needs of others are identified
  - o Triumph is achieved with a solution to their needs

- The keys to success are to have several passions, develop areas of interest that you know more about than others, and use TNT.
- If you want positive results, start written communications with the word "you." That's what the recipient is most interested in.

ON MANAGEMENT

- An employer's highest obligation is to provide meaningful, rewarding work in an atmosphere of civility and respect.
- If you want to test someone's character, don't give them adversity, give them power. How they use power is the true test of character.
- Responsible leaders are careful with their power.
- Unless you've solicited and received "creative disagreement," you probably don't understand all sides of the issue and are not ready to make a decision.
- Experts make as many errors as novices—they have simply become better at catching and correcting them.
- Sometimes the riskiest thing to do is to not take a risk.
- Failure is wasted if you don't take responsibility for it.

MANAGING YOUR EMPLOYEES

- Get good people with the right attitude, expertise, character, and work ethic.
- Coach them regarding your core values to make sure you

are the kind of company you want to be.

- Liberally share information.
- Praise in public, criticize in private.

MAINTAINING YOUR COMPANY AS AN OTHER-CENTERED ORGANIZATION

- See that you provide an outstanding customer experience in all your contacts with customers.
- Ensure that you create inspired rather than just workman-like products.
- Be sure you start all correspondence (emails, letters) with the words "you" or "your," or make sure the customer is at least the subject in the first sentence of your emails and letters. Focus your correspondence on the recipient's needs.
  - o We have found that starting correspondence with the words "you" or "your" has a profound effect on the recipient. Many may not realize, at first, that you are following that policy. But they are more than usually affected by your communications—because they are moved by the realization that the communication is all about them.
  - o One of the benefits of starting with "you" or "your" is that it requires the writer to focus on the needs of the recipient. It's a deliberate exercise for the writer, in that it causes them to spend time considering what the recipient values. The process results in a communication

that is all about the recipient rather than the writer.

ON MANAGING YOURSELF

- Doing things that matter to lots of people means that there will be many opinions of you—and some will be unfavorable no matter how good a job you do.
- You can't control all the things that happen to you, but you can control how you respond to them.
- Anger is a counter-productive and destructive emotion. Attempting to "get it out of your system" by expressing it only prolongs and heightens the emotion.
- Don't take insults and indignities personally—they are a reflection on the other person, not on you.
- Verbal attacks are a compliment; no one will bother to disparage someone who doesn't matter to them.

BECOMING A PERSON EVERYONE WANTS TO KNOW

- One of the greatest rewards you will reap from your habits of PLAY and TNT is the person you will become.
- You will become a knowledgeable leader in your community to whom people will go for leadership.
- Your employees will be proud to work for you.

HAVING FUN

At King Schools, we have fun. We look out for our customers, employees, and vendors. We do everything we can to make the experience of learning to fly a fantastic experience. With the technology of video, we have had the privilege of teaching more pilots than any other ground instructors in the world.

Now it's your turn. You have all the tools and insights to shave years off the entrepreneurial learning curve. It's time for you to start becoming the person you want to be. Everyone you touch will benefit from knowing you.

John & Martha

APPENDIX ONE
MORE ABOUT JOHN AND MARTHA

OUR PARTNERSHIP

When people ask how Martha and I met, I explain that I first dated Martha's older sister and was rejected by her with the words, "You'd really like my sister." When we both became students at Indiana University, Martha's sister arranged for Martha and me to date each other and I found that indeed, I really liked her sister—Martha.

I found Martha to be unassuming, open, and welcoming. When at the end of our first date I told Martha, "I'd like to call you again sometime," Martha replied with a look directly into my eyes and said without posturing, "I'd like that."

One time early in our dating, Martha and I went with my mother to an event in the university stadium. The seats did not have a good view. Martha simply said to me, "I'll be right back," and left with no other comment. When Martha returned she said, "I have better seats for us," and led us to an open area with much better views. I was impressed by the fact that Martha did not complain, she simply presented us with a solution.

Martha and I began to date constantly. My pre-med fraternity brothers said to me, "This is not fair. You and Martha are dating every evening when we have to study full time, while Martha sets the curve in our anatomy class."

It did not take long before Martha and I made a commitment to each other to be equal partners in everything we would do. Martha's major was Comparative Literature, a major which allowed extreme course flexibility. Since my major was accounting, Martha began taking accounting courses to share more with me. By the time we graduated

Martha had more hours of accounting than I did. This served us well—by that time we felt that in order to be equal partners we would need to be entrepreneurs, since it was not probable we could be equal partners working as employees for a company. We pursued a policy of sharing our learning. I took courses in comparative literature to share her interest in that subject. As soon as we were married, we started our first business together and have been equal partners in business ever since.

When we sold our first business I encouraged us to buy an airplane and learn to fly. Martha was not an enthusiastic pilot at first. But soon, when returning at night from a solo cross-country flight, she stepped out of the airplane and said, "That was beautiful!" She had seen the lights on the ground twinkling on and said, "It was like jewels on black velvet." Today one of my lines is, "I want to make it clear, Martha is only a little bit better pilot than I am." My basis of saying that is that Martha is a great risk manager—she is ahead of the airplane and anticipates and manages the risks of flight superbly. My purpose for saying this is to make it clear that our flying partnership, like all the rest of our partnerships, is based on at least equal competence. Today we fly a jet airplane that requires two pilots. It feels like we are dancing a beautiful ballet together.

There was a time period in which I lost my aviation medical. During that time Martha had to recruit and train copilots for our airplane. Meanwhile, I sat in back and watched Martha and her copilot fly. One of my lines was, "I never had a fantasy of watching Martha with other men." My respect for Martha grew during this time period as I saw her manage the entire process with great competence. I told her one time, "I respect and admire you." It got me in trouble with her. I asked, "Why did that make you mad?" She said, "I didn't hear the word love anywhere in that." Scrambling to get out trouble, I said, "I was just trying to explain why I love you."

When flying our Falcon 10 we are totally engaged with each other.

When we decided to teach weekend ground schools for a living I taught private, commercial and flight instructor courses in one meeting room and Martha taught instrument and instrument flight instructor courses in another meeting room. One day at registration, a potential customer realized that Martha would be one of the instructors and whispered to me, "Who will be the instructor for the instrument class?" I replied, "Martha will."

The pilot said, "I had a woman instructor once, and she wasn't very good." After a pause I said, "The odds are that they aren't even related to each other."

I continued, "Let me make a suggestion. Sign up for the course, and if by noon of the first day you aren't happy with the class, leave the class and I'll give you your money back. You will have had one quarter of the class for free."

At noon of the first day, the customer found me and said, "Oh my God, she is fabulous. I am sorry I ever questioned it. You can keep my money. I want to stay."

Martha never takes offense at these kinds of things. She just simply does the job. It has paid off for us for our entire partnership.

As result of teaching weekend ground schools for ten years on a tight schedule, Martha and I had polished our presentation skills—we had learned how to take relatively complicated material and clarify it, simplify it and make it fun. Plus, we developed the use of effective humor to emphasize points and keep attention. When video became available, my uncle said, "You should put your courses on video." My response was, "This just goes to show that you don't know anything about our business—the courses won't work on video." We felt that the outstanding results our students obtained were dependent on the force of our personal presence in the room. My uncle eventually wore us down. We tried video and got a wonderful business result. In effect, what we were able to do is box up John and Martha and ship them off to provide personal ground instruction for aspiring pilots in their kitchens and living rooms. We made very high-quality aviation education accessible to pilots who had not had it before. Flying changed the lives of these pilots, and we had a major influence in doing so—as equal partners.

We have been delivering courses to pilots on video since 1984. Millions of pilots now know us as their personal mentors.

We have been blessed to receive, jointly as equal partners, many awards and honors including from the National Aviation Hall of Fame, which many consider the most prestigious award in aviation. What is most pleasing is the recognition of our partnership.

One of the greatest things about our business and aviation partnership is the personal growth we have each experienced over the decades. We have each learned skills that we did not have when we formed our partnership. For instance, each of us has become a good public speaker. We can make a speech either as individuals or jointly, as we did at the National Aviation Hall of Fame and got a standing ovation from an audience of over 800. We can also, individually or jointly, make polished presentations on video.

It has been a rich and rewarding partnership and marriage. We have grown together and deeply enjoy each other's company. We started our marriage and partnership in 1965 and they are still strong. We think they might last.

John

The ultimate honor for John and Martha was to be
enshrined as the first and only couple in the National
Aviation Hall of Fame.

HOW WE LEARNED TO GET ALONG TOGETHER IN BUSINESS

During the years when we were teaching weekend ground schools, we flew to our venues in a small, twin-engine, pressurized airplane (pilots will want to know it was a Cessna 340). At the time, we were both multi-engine flight instructors and took pride in our flying capability.

We took turns being the pilot flying while the other pilot usually rode in the other front seat.

We had a problem in that the pilot who was not flying would tend to give unsolicited flight instruction to the flying pilot. This resulted in both of us being annoyed. The pilot receiving the unsolicited instruction was annoyed at getting it. The pilot giving the unsolicited instruction was annoyed because it was thoroughly ignored.

We would drive home from the airport in silence, each of us deeply annoyed with the other. Since being pilots and instructors was the core of our lives, this ongoing friction profoundly affected every aspect our partnership.

When we were explaining to a close friend how deeply annoyed each of us was with the other, our friend Bob said, "I can fix that problem for you."

We were both very skeptical. "Bob," we said, "this is too long-lasting and too deep-seated. You are not going to fix it that easily."

Bob said, "Yes I can—and I can do it with one word."

"OK," we finally said, "What's the word?"

Bob said, "The word is "captain." Anytime you feel that you have some advice for the pilot flying, start the sentence with the word captain. And there is more to it," Bob said. "If you want to advise the captain, not only do you start the sentence with the word captain, but you can only give the captain information, not your opinion. For instance, you can say, 'Captain, you are below glidepath; sink 1,000,' but you can't say, 'Martha, you're too damn low.'"

The other side to this is that the captain must not only accept the input, but encourage it.

Bob's advice worked perfectly. We followed it to a T and drove home very satisfied with our flights and very happy with each other. More importantly, we began following that approach in every aspect of our partnership. We had formed the marital and business partnership because we highly respected each other. Not only do we actually use the word "captain" at home and in the business environment, we follow the rule of providing information, but not unsolicited advice. It works like a charm and we get great satisfaction from working with each other.

John

FAA CERTIFICATES AND RATINGS HELD BY BOTH JOHN AND MARTHA

Airline Transport Pilot

- Airplane Single Engine Land
- Airplane Single Engine Sea
- Airplane Multiengine Land
- Airplane Multiengine Sea
- Rotorcraft-Helicopter

Type Ratings

- Falcon 10
- Citation 500
- Citation Mustang 510S
- Eclipse 500S
- LearJet

Commercial Privileges

- Rotorcraft-Gyroplane
- Glider
- Lighter-Than-Air Balloon
- Lighter-Than-Air Airship

Sport Endorsements

- Powered Parachute Land
- Weight-Shift-Control Land

Remote (Drone) Pilot

- Small Unmanned Aircraft System

Flight Instructor

- Airplane Single and Multiengine
- Rotorcraft Helicopter and Gyroplane
- Instrument Airplane and Helicopter
- Glider

CFI Sport Endorsements

- Powered Parachute
- Weight-Shift-Control

FIRST FLIGHT

December 17, 1903, Kitty Hawk, North Carolina

1903   2003

CENTENNIAL COMMISSION

October 31, 2003

Kenneth Mann
Chair

Martha King
The King Companies
3840 Calle Fortunada
San Diego, CA 92123

Dear Ms. King:

On behalf of the First Flight Centennial Commission, we invite you to join us this December at Wright Brothers National Memorial to be honored as one of our distinguished 100 Heroes of Aviation. You and your fellow honorees have been selected from the international aviation community and represent the incredible strides made in aviation and aerospace over the past century. The 100 Heroes program is a focal point in our weeklong celebration of the achievements of Orville and Wilbur Wright and the pioneers who followed in their footsteps. You are one of those pioneers, whose dedication and spirit will inspire generations to continue to reach for the stars.

Your attendance in Kill Devil Hills, North Carolina would include the following opportunities:

- You will be recognized in a ceremony on December 16, which will be open to all visitors at the Centennial celebration.
- You are invited to attend a reception as our honored guest that evening. *16th*
- Please join us as a distinguished guest for the events of December 17, including the reenactment of the First Flight at 10:35 a.m. (second attempt at 2 p.m.).

We hope that you have already made arrangements to be in attendance for this historic occasion, however we are happy to assist in facilitating your travel plans and accommodations if those are not already in place.

It would be our great pleasure to host you as an honored guest for this extraordinary event. Given your role as one of the 100 Heroes of Aviation, your presence would certainly enrich this celebration of one of the most significant achievements of humankind. We feel that the commemoration of the triumphs of the Wright Brothers and their legacy of aviation, in which you play an integral role, is of the utmost importance, given the tremendous impact of flight on the past century. There is no better locale to celebrate these achievements than the very place where manned, powered, sustained, controlled flight began.

Please contact Kim Sawyer in response to this request. She can be reached by phone at 252-441-6291 ext. 225 or via email at KimSawyer2003nc@earthlink.net. Upon your reply, we will contact you with further details concerning you participation. We hope that you will be able to be with us, and congratulations again on your historic successes.

*Katie
Lilly
ex 228*

Sincerely,

Ken Mann
Chairman, First Flight Centennial Commission

Telephone: 252/441-6291 • Fax: 252/441-5462
800 Colington Road, Kill Devil Hills 27948
Mailing Address: Post Office Box 1903, Kill Devil Hills, North Carolina 27948-1903
www.firstflightnc.com

An Equal Opportunity/Affirmative Action Employer

John was shocked when he first realized that Martha had made notes on the original of the letter she received.

The presidential appointment makes an impressive display.

FLYING THE BLIMP

The chief pilot of the FujiFilm blimp had great advice for us: "Don't ever promise a ride in the blimp unless you are absolutely sure you can deliver it. The person you promised it to will never forget it."

John and I were chosen to fly the FujiFilm blimp because of our unusual flying experience. We were already helicopter pilots and float-plane pilots. Each of those are often operated without the benefit of hard surface runways. So are blimps. Our off-runway experience was useful in blimp flying, as was the wind awareness we developed as float-plane and helicopter pilots.

Captaining a blimp is an exercise in crew resource management. A crew of eighteen traveled with the FujiFilm blimp and a ground crew assisted with every takeoff and landing. Our jobs were to protect the safety of the blimp, its crew, and its passengers as we operated from an open field near an airport runway. The ground crew were at risk of being dragged or lifted into the air by the blimp as we took off and landed.

Although it seems counterintuitive, captaining a blimp is the most difficult and complicated thing we have done in aviation. Helicopters require lots of skill to fly, but unlike blimps, at least they do what you ask them to do. Blimps simply are not that responsive to control inputs. Plus, you have the complexity of taking care of all the people in the operation.

Also counterintuitive is that blimps are just about the most exhilarating thing we have ever flown. The blimp took us to exciting events and places. We have flown the FujiFilm blimp over the Kentucky Derby, the Super Bowl, the U.S. Tennis Open, downtown New York City, San Francisco over the Golden Gate Bridge, and the length of the

California coast. As husband-and-wife blimp captains we have been the subject of many conversations by sports announcers on TV. Plus, every person we have given a ride to on the blimp will remember it to their dying day. It is one of those very special experiences our passion for flying opened up for us.

Martha

When you give someone a ride in a blimp, they will remember it forever.

John and Martha became seaplane instructors early in their flying careers.

FLYING OUR OWN AIRPLANE

As we have progressed in our aviation business, we have always traveled using our own airplane for transportation.

Personal flying means different things to different people. But for nearly everyone, flying represents a profound expression of freedom. It gives us the ability to leave the earth, take command of the third dimension, and explore our world from above.

For us, using our airplanes as our vehicles for personal transportation has allowed us to extend that freedom even further. With our own airplane we have the ability to travel to the places, and at the times, of our own choosing. Within days after earning our private pilot certificates in our first airplane, a Cherokee 140, we headed from our Indiana home down to Florida and the Bahamas.

On our way back north, the first appearance of snow on the ground in Tennessee prompted us to exercise our newfound freedom by immediately turning left to go explore the California coast. The aerial tour resulted in our discovering a little Southern California seaside town that resonated with us. We have lived in La Jolla, California, ever since.

It wasn't long before we hungered for more speed and more range, and we gained wider horizons with the purchase of our Piper Comanche. In our first year of flying the Comanche, we experienced the breathtaking vista as we crested the mountain range north of Acapulco and viewed the sparkling bay and the dramatically beautiful expanse of the sea. Within that same year we also made the mind-opening trip to Barrow, Alaska, the northernmost city in the United States.

Through the years, except for some international trips, we have always flown our own airplane for transportation, and, whenever money allowed, stepped up to faster and longer-legged aerial steeds.

Of course, it should be no surprise that you can travel around the country much more cheaply on the airlines than in a general aviation airplane. That hasn't always been the case. Back when we were traveling in our single-engine Comanche, if we had two people in the airplane we could fly coast to coast for the same price as on the airlines. But today, if the only consideration were money, going economy class on the airlines would win hands down.

Next, when it comes to time, in most cases the airlines win. But not always—it depends on how fast your airplane is and whether the airliner is going where you want to go. But when you figure in the extra time you have to allow to compensate for possible traffic delays and then the extra time for getting in and out of the airline terminal, the calculation changes in favor of flying your own airplane. Plus, there are the benefits in personal flying of traveling according to your own schedule, not that of the airlines, and doing it without the crowds.

But what has motivated us to use general aviation airplanes for our personal transportation is neither money nor time. It has been the experience. We actively enjoy every minute of the experience of flying our own airplane. It makes us eager to take business trips when otherwise we'd look for excuses not to go. When we fly our own airplane, it is not unusual for us to get back from an important business trip, and on the drive home the conversation is all about how fun the flight was rather than about the business.

Even though flying is challenging, every aspect of it from the pre-flight planning to the management of the airplane in flight is deeply rewarding.

John and Martha

JOHN AND MARTHA'S AWARDS AND HONORS

- 2021 John and Martha were jointly inducted into the Flight Instructor Hall of Fame. Its purpose is to recognize those individuals who have made significant contributions to aviation education and flight instruction while reflecting credit upon themselves and their profession.

- 2019 John and Martha were jointly enshrined in the National Aviation Hall of Fame (NAHF) Class of 2019. Each year, the NAHF selects five or six inductees from a prestigious group of over 300 previously nominated air and space pioneers to be recognized for their achievements during what is described as "The Oscar Night of Aviation." Their joint selection as husband and wife is unprecedented.

- 2019 John and Martha were jointly inducted into the Organization of Black Aerospace Professionals (OBAP) Founders and Pioneers Hall of Fame in recognition of their lifelong dedication to making aviation accessible to all.

- 2019 John and Martha jointly received the Jack J. Eggspuehler Award from the National Association of Flight Instructors (NAFI). This award honors individuals or organizations that have made a significant contribution to flight instructors, flight instruction, or aviation education.

- 2019 John and Martha were jointly chosen as one of "Eight Who Made It Great—the most inspirational personalities in general aviation," based on an online survey of AOPA members. The others named were Bob Hoover, John Glenn, Chuck Yeager,

Burt Rutan, Elrey Jeppesen, Paul Poberezny, and Bill Lear.

- 2018 John and Martha jointly received the Distinguished Statesman of Aviation award by the National Aeronautic Association (NAA). The award honors outstanding living Americans who, by their efforts over an extended period of years, have made contributions of significant value to aeronautics and have reflected credit upon the United States and themselves.

- 2018 Martha was appointed jointly by the Secretary of the Air Force and the national commander of the Civil Air Patrol to the Board of Governors. Founded on December 1, 1941, to help protect the nation's shorelines from German U-boats, CAP has evolved into a premier public service organization using more than 560 general aviation airplanes.

- 2017 John and Martha were jointly awarded the Crystal Eagle Award by the Aero Club of Northern California in honor of their significant contributions to the advancement of aviation. Previous awardees include Jimmy Doolittle, Chuck Yeager, Stanly Hiller, Bill Lear, Eileen Collins, and Julie Clark.

- 2017 Martha received the Women in Leadership award from the San Diego East County Chamber of Commerce. The award is presented to San Diego County residents who have demonstrated exemplary character, integrity, and outstanding leadership, not only in their field but also in their community.

- 2015 John and Martha were jointly awarded the Pinnacle Award by the Flight School Association of North America for their years of service to the general aviation industry.

- 2014 Martha King was selected by the Ohio School Board Association as a "Proud Product of Ohio Public Schools," a graduate who has achieved great success in their chosen field.
- 2014 John was awarded the Wright Brothers Master Pilot Award by the FAA for having demonstrated professionalism, skill, and aviation expertise for more than fifty years.
- 2014 John and Martha were jointly awarded the Sword of Honour by the Honourable Company of Air Pilots for outstanding contributions to general aviation. The presentation was made by His Royal Highness Prince Michael of Kent in the ancient Guildhall of London.
- 2014 John and Martha were jointly honored by Tomorrow's Aeronautical Museum with the "Inspiring and Educating Aviators" award.
- 2014 John was named by AOPA's *Pilot* magazine as one of twenty-four "General Aviation Giants" whose "contributions influence the way we fly and think about flying."
- 2012 John and Martha were jointly awarded the prestigious Frank G. Brewer Trophy for Aviation Education by the National Aeronautic Association (NAA) for their significant contributions of enduring value to aerospace education by making aviation knowledge more accessible to pilots worldwide.
- 2012 John and Martha were jointly awarded the IAOPA Service Award for Excellence in Aviation Safety and Pilot Training Education by the International Council of Aircraft Owner and Pilot Associations at the 26th World Assembly, Cape Town, South Africa.

- 2012 John and Martha were both named "Living Legends of Aviation" in an exciting evening in Beverly Hills sponsored by the Kiddie Hawk Air Academy, joining a short list of aviation luminaries that includes Bob Hoover, Clay Lacy, Harrison Ford, Morgan Freeman, Kurt Russell, Tom Cruise, and "Sully" Sullenberger.

- 2011 Martha was named chairman of the Chancellor's Community Advisory Board, University of California San Diego. The board is composed of citizens of the community interested in fostering positive and productive relationships between UC San Diego and the community at large.

- 2010 Martha was inducted into the Fairborn (Ohio) Schools Hall of Honor, which recognizes the outstanding achievements of graduates of Fairborn Schools.

- 2009 John and Martha were jointly awarded the American Spirit Award by the National Business Aviation Association. This award is presented in recognition of individuals within business aviation who exemplify the courage and pursuit of excellence and service to others that characterizes the men and women who created and nurtured the American aviation community.

- 2008 John and Martha were inducted as a couple into the International Aerospace Hall of Fame. They joined famous aviation pioneers such as the Wright Brothers, Charles Lindbergh, Chuck Yeager, Jack Northrop, William Boeing, Reuben H. Fleet, Glenn Curtiss, Wally Schirra, T. Claude Ryan, and Jimmy Doolittle Jr.

- 2008 John and Martha each received the prestigious Lowell Thomas Award from The Explorers Club. This award is named for Explorers Club member Lowell Thomas, the journalist whose news reports introduced "Lawrence of Arabia" (T. E. Lawrence) to the Western public. The award is given to honor men and women who have distinguished themselves in the field of exploration. John and Martha were recognized for their work in making aviation accessible as a tool for exploration.

- 2008 John and Martha were each elected as Fellows of the Explorers Club in New York City for their contributions to the cause of exploring by making aviation accessible as a tool for exploration throughout the world.

- 2008 John and Martha jointly received the Vision Award from Business & Commercial Aviation. Other 2008 recipients include Michimasa Fujino, CEO of Honda Aircraft Company and the driving force behind the Honda Jet, and Paul Bowen, the inspirational artistic aviation air-to-air photographer.

- 2008 John and Martha jointly received the Forrest M. and Pamela Bird award by the Civil Aviation Medical Association for "exceptional contributions to the safety of civil aviation as pilots and educators through exercising excellent judgment, logic and common sense in evaluation and training of civil pilots through the years."

- 2007 John and Martha received honorary Paul Tissandier Diplomas from the Fédération Aéronautique Internationale (FAI), in Lausanne, Switzerland, for serving the cause of general aviation through "their work, initiative, and devotion."

- 2007 John was named Chairman of the Board of the Charles A. and Anne Morrow Lindbergh Foundation. John and Martha both serve on the board. The Foundation, established in 1977 through the leadership of Neil Armstrong and Jimmy Doolittle, strives to improve the quality of human life by inspiring a balance between technology and our environment.

- 2005 Martha was awarded the prestigious Cliff Henderson Award for Achievement from the National Aeronautic Association. This annual award is presented to "a living individual or group whose vision, leadership, or skill has made a significant and lasting contribution to the promotion and advancement of aviation or space activity." Previous recipients include Jimmy Doolittle, Roscoe Turner, General Curtis LeMay, Frank Borman, Scott Crossfield, Anne Morrow Lindbergh, and Ernest K. Gann.

- 2004 John and Martha were each presented with "Master Air Pilot" awards in recognition of long service and consistently high standards by the Guild of Air Pilots and Air Navigators in a ceremony presided over by His Royal Highness Prince Andrew, Duke of York, in the ancient Guildhall of London.

- 2004 John received the 2004 "Excellence in Pilot Training" award from the National Air Transportation Association.

- 2003 Martha was named one of the "100 Most Influential Women in Aviation" by Women in Aviation International.

- 2003 Martha honored as one of the 100 Distinguished Aviation Heroes in the first century of flight by the First Flight

Centennial Commission. At Kitty Hawk on December 16, 2003, Martha shared this honor with Neil Armstrong, Buzz Aldrin, Chuck Yeager, John Glenn, Patty Wagstaff, and fifteen others of the thirty-two recipients still living.

- 2003 Martha was honored by a resolution of the California Assembly and a proclamation from the governor of California as the EAA chose Martha to fly the state flag to Kitty Hawk for the First Flight Centennial.

- 2002 John and Martha were inducted into the International Forest of Friendship for contributions to aviation. The International Forest of Friendship is in Atchison, Kansas, hometown of Amelia Earhart.

- 2001 Martha was appointed by President Clinton to the First Flight Centennial Federal Advisory Board to help promote celebrations of the 100th anniversary of flight.

- 1996 John and Martha were named "Aviation Educators of the Year" by *Professional Pilot* magazine.

LEARNING HOW TO EXTEND OURSELVES TO PEOPLE WE DON'T KNOW

When people you have never met before start recognizing you, it can be a very uncomfortable experience. If you have played a role in their lives that is important to them, such as teaching them flying on video, they get very excited when they see you. When you have strangers start hugging you and jumping up and down with excitement when they see you, you don't feel that you can match their excitement and don't know what to do.

If you don't respond favorably to the attention, they are very unhappy. But you are not prepared to respond, there is no place to go to learn how to do it.

One time at an airshow, a man who had obviously been drinking approached Martha. He felt entitled to a positive response from her and became angry when Martha withdrew.

Another time I immediately retreated into our hotel room when female jumpers surprised me as I stepped into the hall.

Finally, we had a conference with each other and talked about the fact that our responses just weren't working. We discussed this with a friend who had met Bill Clinton. Our friend explained that Clinton had clasped his hand and pulled our friend toward himself while looking him intently in the eye, then spent sixty seconds talking to him before moving on.

We decided that was what we needed to do. But we would go even further—we would put energy into the meeting and make it all about them. We developed the habit of looking our new friends in the eye and asking them all about their flying. It works marvelously. Folks are much happier now after meeting us than people were previously.

If only we could figure out how to make this all less fatiguing.

John

MAGIC JOHNSON

Since retiring as an extraordinary professional basketball player, Magic Johnson has become an entrepreneur, philanthropist, broadcaster and motivational speaker. As an entrepreneur and frequent user of business aircraft, Magic was selected as the keynote speaker for the 2019 National Business Aviation Conference (NBAA).

The meeting planners spent great effort to provide a striking venue for him including ideal lighting. At the very start of his talk Magic foiled their plans by leaping off the stage and out of the spotlights to greet attendees personally. With a 6' 9" stature, his plan was to dramatically contrast his great height with a diminutive audience member. He selected Martha, a mere 5'1", from the front row of the audience. Despite her small size, Martha displayed confidence and warmth as she and Magic posed together. Many in the audience realized that Magic had made an extraordinary choice by unwittingly selecting a member of the National Aviation Hall of Fame. It was a memorable event for the pilots in the audience who were very familiar with Martha.

John

Martha has great stature as John's business partner, not so much physically.

SPACE SHUTTLE FLIGHTS

One of the great aviation experiences is seeing a space shuttle launch up close and personally. We have been fortunate to have the experience twice. Once was from the VIP area due to our close association with the American Radio Relay League as a consequence of providing video courses for them. They were able to provide VIP access because they had a youth program in which youth talked to astronauts in space by amateur radio.

Our second close experience of a shuttle launch was from the press area as a result of our relationship with CNN.

The most surprising thing about seeing the launches was the brightness of them. It appeared as if we were looking directly at a welder's torch. The second surprising thing was how the thunder of the engines actually rumbled throughout our bodies.

Additionally, we saw and heard the space shuttle on landing approach when we were flying the FujiFilm blimp in Orlando, Florida. The double sonic boom shook the entire ship—we thought at first we had had a structural failure. Plus, one time we flew our airplane to the airspace next to Edwards Air Force Base, and saw from the air the space shuttle landing on the dry lakebed. It was an exhilarating way to follow our passion for aviation.

Martha

One of the great aviation experiences is seeing a space shuttle launch up close and personally.

MICROSOFT FLIGHT SIMULATOR

In 2004, Microsoft Flight Simulator opened with a screenshot of me sitting at a computer running Flight Simulator and Martha looking over my shoulder. My role was to fail to read the instructions and to make a lot of mistakes, and Martha's role was to have read the instructions and to keep trying to straighten me out—a nearly hopeless assignment.

This all started when Microsoft came to Martha and me and said, "We are having too many people give up on Flight Simulator. Do you think you could create a fun video that people would watch and from it learn to fly the program successfully?"

This is how we became recognized all over the world by simulator fans and watched on video in seven different languages. Our job was to make the program feel doable and fun—people all over the world told us we got it done.

John

APPENDIX TWO
PEOPLE JOHN AND MARTHA
HAVE MET THROUGH AVIATION ENTREPRENEURSHIP

DICK SMITH OF AUSTRALIA

We got to know Dick Smith and his wife Pip because of our mutual interest in flying. We originally met Dick at a helicopter convention in Anaheim, California. Dick is a helicopter owner and pilot as well as an airplane owner and pilot. His first direction in life was as an entrepreneur. He founded a consumer electronics brand, Dick Smith Electronics, which still has hundreds of stores in Australia and New Zealand. The brand features a caricature of Dick's portrait with glasses. As a result, Dick is famous throughout Australia and New Zealand.

When Dick learned to fly helicopters in his 30s he began adventuring in support of Australia Geographic, which he founded after he sold Dick Smith Electronics. He set many records, including completing the first solo helicopter flight around the world and the first helicopter flight to the North Pole. Later, Dick flew a Twin Otter airplane on a trip around the world—not horizontally, around the equator, but vertically, over both poles—during which he landed at both the North and South Poles. Dick has continued a lifetime of adventuring by aircraft. Martha and I have been fortunate to be included in some of these trips, even being incorporated as pilots.

As an extremely successful entrepreneur, Dick has been able to richly serve society. He has done so as an innovative thought leader, as chairman of Australia's Civil Aviation Safety Authority, and as a philanthropist, with contributions to Australia's CARE to support worker human rights in Vietnam. Due to our mutual interests in aviation and entrepreneurship, we have enjoyed a long and rewarding friendship with Dick and Pip.

John

Dick was a pioneer at using helicopters to take him
to extraordinary places like the North Pole.

PHIL BOYER

Phil Boyer is an aviation leader who, as president of the Aircraft Owners and Pilots Association, grew it to record levels, brought the aviation community together, and provided an unprecedented sense of direction for the entire aviation community. Previously, Phil had been an executive with ABC. As such, Phil had run several of ABC's company-owned TV stations. He eventually became the general manager of all the company-owned stations. Later Phil became the manager of entertainment programming for ABC.

Throughout his entire career, Phil's passion for flying was obvious. Through the years Phil owned airplanes and became a knowledgeable and competent pilot. While with ABC Phil started and ran a business for them titled ABC's *Wide World of Flying*. It was a subscription service of very high-quality videos featuring aviation and flying. We got to know Phil when our office manager came in and said, "I have someone on the phone who claims to be Vice President of ABC." We took the call and found Phil to be strikingly competent. We became familiar with the video program and were impressed. Martha and I made video presentations in it and became advertisers. As a result, we got to know Phil and pursued our mutual interest in flying (Phil owned and flew the same kind of airplane we had at the time—a Cessna 340—which Phil was planning to fly across the North Atlantic to Europe).

We recommended Phil for president of AOPA to the Chairman of AOPA's Board when the previous president of AOPA was about to leave. Phil made a great impression on the Board chairman but asked to delay his interview with the Board as a whole so he could complete his dream flight across the North Atlantic first. We were disappointed in the delay, but eventually realized that it helped confirm Phil's passion for flying and strengthened the Board's interest in him.

Our friendship with Phil and Lois Boyer took us to a lot of fun events including dinner in front of the Parthenon during the International Aircraft Owners and Pilots Association meeting in Athens.

Through the years our relationship with Phil and his wife, Lois (who is also a pilot), strengthened. We enjoyed skiing trips together and other vacations. They are great intellectual companions. We share a mutual interest in entrepreneurship and marketing. We have learned a lot from Phil over the years and greatly appreciate the friendship of both Phil and Lois.

Our regard for Phil is so high that when we were to be enshrined in the National Aviation Hall of Fame, we asked him to introduce us. Phil gave a fun and playful introduction, revealing intimacies that provided the audience with a warm familiarity with us. We are waiting for the opportunity to retaliate.

John and Martha

BETTY FORD

Dagmar Dolby was sponsoring an event to which she invited Betty Ford to speak. When Dagmar spoke to Mrs. Ford, the former First Lady said she would be delighted to speak, but she did not want to fly on a commercial airliner. The Dolbys asked if we would be willing to fly Mrs. Ford from Palm Springs to San Francisco and back. It sounded like a very special experience to us, so we immediately said yes.

It was a project. The Secret Service said they needed to interview us. We flew to Palm Springs for the interview. Surprisingly, it was fun. We didn't know what the purpose of the interview was, but it appeared to us that they just wanted to get to know us. There were no challenging or threatening questions. It was apparent that they already knew a huge amount about us. We imagine they just didn't want any surprises.

On the day of the trip, the Secret Service folks showed up early. They were personable, appropriate, and professional. An agent went on board with a large backpack and set it on a sideways seat by the door. John said, "I suppose I shouldn't ask what's in the bag." The agent said, "You don't want to know." We left it at that. In San Francisco, as Mrs. Ford and we left the airplane, a man approached John and said, "We'll take care of your airplane, sir." John's first reaction was to think, "You keep away from our airplane." Then John realized the man was wearing a wire and recognized who it must be and why he said it. Once again, we left it at that.

On the return to Palm Springs, much to our chagrin, Mrs. Ford slipped on the overly polished steps as she left the airplane. As John saw Mrs. Ford walking away, he said, "I'm glad to see her rear." I said, "Aw, why did you say that? She was wonderful." John responded, "It was a lot of responsibility." It was, indeed, a wonderful experience.

Martha

Betty Ford could not have been more kind and gracious.

BILL AND GAYLE COOK

We got to know Bill and Gayle Cook due to our mutual interests in flying and in entrepreneurship. Bill and Gayle had founded Cook, Inc., which was developing cardiovascular catheters for the then-experimental procedure known as an angiogram. Flying was an important part of their business since they used airplanes to visit interventional cardiology pioneers and to frequently bring them back to the factory. The procedures were life-preserving and became an important part of the practice of cardiology.

Over the years, Martha and I came to know the Cooks as influential in cardiology, but we were not fully aware that they had become billionaires and influential leaders in their home state of Indiana. One of the interests the Cooks had was architectural preservation. This led them to restore the courthouse square of their headquarters town, Bloomington, Indiana, and many other places in the area. Plus, they restored many historical places around the state, including hotels in French Lick and West Baden as well as a plantation near the Ohio River. As part of their passion about architectural preservation they became experts in the restoration of historic domes, including the 200-foot-diameter dome at the West Baden Springs Hotel—at the time it was built, the largest dome in the world.

Other interests included supporting a drum and bugle corps group called the Star of Indiana, in appreciation of the benefits they saw accrue to their son, Carl. Bill not only provided financing, but he also drove busses personally for their transportation.

With support from the Cooks, the Star became a champion corps.

In 1999, Star premiered the stage show Blast! at the Hammersmith Theatre in London, England. Its audience steadily grew until it became a top ten hit on the London stage. After a year in London, Blast! returned to the United States in 2000, debuting on the Broadway stage to rave reviews. The show won the 2001 Tony Award for Best Special Theatrical Event, and, when it was videotaped for PBS, won the 2001 Emmy Award for Best Choreography. After its Broadway run, Star took *Blast!* on the road, with companies touring the country each year to large and enthusiastic audiences. Casts were also developed to perform long-term engagements at Disneyland in Anaheim, California, and at Disney World in Orlando, Florida. *Blast!* continued to tour through 2012.

Successful entrepreneur Bill Cook (L) and his Chief Pilot Bob Harbstreit (R) became and remained close friends.

Bill and Gayle Cook are a wonderful example of how entrepreneurs with lots of passion and many interests become wonderful contributors to many communities.

John

BILL BRODY, PRESIDENT OF SALK INSTITUTE

One day Martha and I were picking up our airplane after maintenance, and another pilot and his instructor spotted us and came over from their single-engine turboprop to talk with us. This is always a great pleasure for us. Pilots usually have lots of interests and are generally very interesting people. Pus, they are very passionate about their flying. Many of them have used our courses and are eager to meet us. We always have lots to talk about.

This pilot, Bill Brody, was learning to fly his turboprop and had taken our courses for years. We could have talked with each other for the rest of the day. Bill was a radiologist, a former president of Johns Hopkins University, and at that time president of the Salk Institute.

We did indeed have plenty to talk about, and Bill invited us to come visit with him at Salk. We wound up visiting with him frequently. Bill was interested in the subject of risk management, which we had developed courses on for the aviation community, and he invited us to speak on the subject in the Salk Institute auditorium.

As is often the case, our business of teaching pilots introduces us to very engaged people who greatly expand our lives.

John

CHUCK YEAGER

Chuck Yeager liked women who fly. Among those was Jacqueline Cochran. Chuck Yeager helped make airplanes available to Jackie that allowed her to set a speed record in an F-86 and become the first woman to go supersonic.

Another female pilot Chuck Yeager liked was Martha. Chuck invited Martha to every celebration he could think of. He arranged for Martha to land among U2s at Beale Air Force Base for his birthday. Plus, he arranged for Martha to land at Edwards Air Force Base for the dedication of Chuck's statue at Sound Barrier Park.

Even though Chuck was a one-star general, he had an antipathy for higher rank, including four-star generals. One time at a dinner given by a four-star general, Chuck and Martha were sitting next to each other and Chuck was telling Martha a story. When the four-star general got up to the podium to give his speech, Chuck continued with his story. It could be thought that Martha was getting Chuck into trouble. But the truth was, Chuck didn't need Martha's help to get into trouble. One of Check's senior officers told us, "You did always have to fly high cover for him."

John

Chuck Yeager was famously informal.

CLINT EASTWOOD

Clint was learning to fly helicopters. His instructor told us Clint was a fine helicopter pilot, but he was having difficulty with ground school. He needed to pass his FAA knowledge test soon so he could get his pilot certificate, which would enable him to fly helicopters in Africa while he made the movie *White Hunter, Black Heart*.

We do ground instruction very well. But we needed undistracted privacy for him to learn quickly before he went Africa. So we invited Clint to stay with us in our house while we gave him the ground school he needed. Clint was a delight to work with. He was polite and soft-spoken. When we took breaks, Clint would go over to our piano and play and sing. He is very musical and has a great voice.

The privacy was absolutely essential for Clint to learn well. On the one occasion when we went out to eat, he had to put out extra effort to respond to fans. We decided from then on we would order in and avoid the distractions.

Clint got his pilot certificate and was able to fly helicopters in Africa. He sent us a wonderful letter that we have framed in our office.

Martha

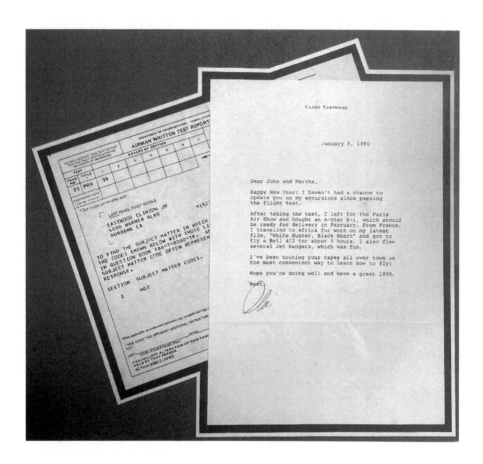

Clint Eastwood in life is the opposite of his "Dirty Harry" image.

ERIK LINDBERGH, GRANDSON OF CHARLES LINDBERGH

At the age of twenty-five, Charles Lindbergh changed the world view of aviation by flying solo from New York to Paris nonstop May 20–21, 1927.

Decades later, Charles's grandson Erik Lindbergh used King Schools courses to pursue his own love of aviation. When Erik wanted to commemorate the seventy-fifth anniversary of his grandfather's flight, he decided the best way to do it was to himself fly solo and nonstop from New York to Paris. Erik asked John and me to help him manage the risks of making the trip.

Consequently, we helped with Erik's flight planning and monitored the progress of his flight, which Erik conducted successfully in May 2002. Today, John and I are on the board of the Lindbergh Foundation, which continues the legacy of Charles and Anne Morrow Lindbergh's lifetime of service by spearheading bold solutions and inspiring talent to help balance technology and the environment.

Martha

John and Martha send Erik Lindbergh off on his quest to recreate his grandfather's solo non-stop flight from New York to Paris.

After sending Erik Lindbergh off to recreate his grandfather's flight from New York to Paris, John and Martha flew their plane to Mission Control in St. Louis to monitor the flight.

HARRISON FORD

Our aviation link is a powerful connection to anybody engaged in aviation—including Harrison Ford. Like us, Harrison is both an airplane and a helicopter pilot. Consequently, when Harrison spots Martha at an aviation event, he gives her little peck on the forehead. We have enjoyed dinner with Harrison and Calista and countless evenings celebrating aviation with Harrison and other aviation friends. He is always gracious and generous.

As a celebrity who flies, any slight aviation mistake Harrison makes receives international publicity. We have always admired the way Harrison handles these events. He immediately takes responsibility and is open and straightforward.

We have watched Harrison deal with the crushing attention he gets when he is out in public. When we commented on the gracious and kind way he deals with everybody, he said, "It's my job." From our perspective, it's a lot of work.

John

Harrison Ford is a genuine aviation enthusiast.

NEIL ARMSTRONG AND THE FIRST FLIGHT CENTENNIAL COMMISSION

December 3, 2003, was the hundredth anniversary of the first flight at Kitty Hawk by Wilbur and Orville Wright. Martha was stunned when she received a letter from the First Flight Centennial Commission telling her that she was to be honored as one of one hundred distinguished aviation heroes at the anniversary event in Kitty Hawk. Other honorees were to include Neil Armstrong, Chuck Yeager, Bob Hoover, and Buzz Aldrin.

When Martha realized she was to speak at the event, she saw this as a great honor but also a responsibility to attend. She started using a yellow marker to highlight items on the letter and used a ballpoint pen to make notes in the margin. My comment was, "Martha, what are you doing? You are going to want to frame this letter! Then I realized that Martha's markings showed that her sense of responsibility overshadowed her sense of self-importance. I later understood that Martha's markings actually increased the value of the letter.

In connection with the event, Martha received a presidential appointment from Bill Clinton to the First Flight Centennial Federal Advisory Board. Our office staff tried to be casual as they inquired, "Martha, did you get the message from the White House?"

Another member of the board was Neil Armstrong, who shared Martha's interest in teaching. Over several meetings they got to know each other pretty well. When Neil would see her at an event, he would come over to say hi. One time on a bus, Neil reached over Martha to shake hands with me and introduce himself. I saw it as Neil's way to make a gift to Martha. Through the years, neither Martha nor I talked with Neil about his time with NASA. Whenever I saw him I called him "professor," which was obviously pleasing to him.

John

Neal Armstrong was warm and unpretentious.

RAY DOLBY

He could have been a ten-year-old kid—he was certainly acting like one. We were at the Helicopter Association International annual convention and John was sitting in a helicopter pretending to fly it. He gradually became aware that someone had been standing beside him waiting for him to come out of his fantasy. "I am so sorry," John said. "I just realized you've been waiting to get into the helicopter."

"No," the patient man said, "I've been waiting to talk to you."

The man waiting had recently used our courses in his studying to learn to fly and he wanted to explain that we had helped him with something that meant the world to him. As the conversation progressed, John began to realize that this very expressive, personable man was an extraordinary person. "I'm John King," John said as he extended his hand. "I'm Ray Dolby," the good-natured man replied. John can be slow on the uptake at times, and it took him a while to realize that this was the Dolby who had created the noise-reduction system and the company that was known worldwide for extraordinary innovations in audio systems.

As John and Ray talked about flying, Ray explained that he had discovered flying late in life and deeply regretted the many years he hadn't been experiencing the joy of flight. Ray was now in a hurry to drink deeply from the well of satisfaction and fulfillment that flying provides.

As John and Ray talked, they realized that they had much more to talk about than the circumstances allowed. Ray invited us to spend a weekend with him and his wife, Dagmar, at their Lake Tahoe vacation home. There we discovered that this was a person with deep passions not only about flying, but about many subjects. He had lots of interests, and even in his seventies was always learning. These were habits he'd had all his life, and they served him well. They certainly made him interesting company. We became friends and did many things together, including taking flying vacations. We never ran out of fascinating things to talk about. It was a relationship we continued to enjoy greatly right up until Ray passed away.

John and Martha with Ray Dolby
and son David after a great dinner.

We knew what Ray meant to us—he was a great friend and a fabulous intellectual companion. But it wasn't until we attended his celebration of life that we began to realize what Ray meant to the rest of the world. He had improved the quality of sound experienced in movies, symphonies, music discs, and every other form of music so significantly that people in those communities referred to time as BD and AD— "Before Dolby" and "After Dolby." At his memorial service, representatives of each of these communities were there to explain how Ray had improved their world.

When John and I read the articles about Ray afterwards, we began to fully understand he was an enormous success in about every way you could measure—including his contributions to the communities he served and in his financial accomplishments. We had never considered that he was a billionaire.

This made us very thoughtful. There are not that many billionaires around, but as we began to think about it, we realized that we knew more than a few. Why did we know so many billionaires? Because we had spent our lives teaching, talking about, and living and breathing flying. Flying attracts successful, motivated winners, and, we believe, supports them in becoming even more successful.

Martha

REEVE LINDBERGH

As people who are known by pilots around the world, John and I are members of the Lindbergh Foundation Board and John was formerly chairman. In those positions we did of course get to know the other members of the Lindbergh Board.

Among the most notable is the ever warm and gracious Reeve Lindbergh, the youngest child of Charles and Anne Morrow Lindbergh. Like her mother, Reeve is a very thoughtful and engaging author. Much of what Reeve writes about is growing up as the daughter of what was, at the time, one of the most famous couples in the world.

A cute story that Reeve told us is of taking her young teenage son to the National Air and Space Museum on the Mall in Washington, D.C., to see her father's famous airplane, the *Spirit of St. Louis*—the plane he flew solo and nonstop from New York to Paris in 1927. The plane was hanging from the ceiling. When Reeve's son came down from the plane, Reeve asked him what he thought of the experience. He said, "That was cool. I've never been in a cherry-picker before."

Getting to know the Lindberghs is another great example of how entrepreneurship opens the world to you.

Martha

ROBERT POOLEY AND QUEEN NOOR OF JORDAN

Entrepreneurship in aviation has opened up many opportunities for us to meet special people. One such person was Robert Pooley, who walked in the front door at King Schools asking to meet John and Martha. Robert was a delight for us to get to know. He was an aviation entrepreneur from England and owned Pooley's Flight Equipment. He was in the business of supplying pilots the essential information they needed for aviation cross-country trips, information that was not available on UK aviation navigation charts. In the United States, that information is provided by the government in a publication then called the "Airport/Facility Directory," now referred to as the "Chart Supplement."

Robert lives life to the fullest. He is well-known for flying hot air balloons and gave Queen Noor of Jordan a ride in his balloon. He caused a great stir when he surprised her security detail with an unexpected route. Unexpected routes are, of course, usual in balloon flying because balloons are not steerable. You select your route by picking an altitude with winds that will, hopefully, take you where you want to go.

Robert's entrepreneurship caused him to buy and restore Forter Castle in the Scottish Highlands. Today you can book the castle to conduct your own event.

Robert extended his entrepreneurship by purchasing the famed sword line of Wilkinson Sword, which supplies swords to the British armed forces as well as other military units around the world. They also make ceremonial swords. One such sword, the Sword of Honour, was awarded jointly to John and me in 2014 by the Honourable Company of Air Pilots for outstanding contributions to general aviation. The presentation was made by His Royal Highness, The Prince Michael of Kent, in the ancient Guildhall of London.

In January 2016, Robert received an MBE (Most Excellent Order of the British Empire).

Martha

ALEXANDER ZUYEV, RUSSIAN FIGHTER PILOT

On multiple occasions, Russian pilots have announced that they use our videos. In one case an AN-225, often considered the largest plane in the world, flew in to a popular general aviation airshow in Oshkosh, Wisconsin. The pilots sought us out and invited us into the cockpit. It was huge. There were stations for two pilots, a flight engineer, a communications officer, and a navigator. It resembled a huge oceangoing ship.

The pilots bought dozens of our video courses and flew them back to Russia in the plane.

One day a man walked into our offices and announced that he was Alexander Zuyev and that he was the last Russian pilot to defect from Russia in a MiG-29 Fulcrum jet. He claimed, "All the MiG-29 pilots I know use your courses." The basis for the statement was that they were all hoping to fly with a U.S. airline and were using our courses to prepare for their U.S. exams. Zuyev later wrote a book titled *Fulcrum: A Top Gun Pilot's Escape from the Soviet Empire.*
Martha

CNN AND WALTER CRONKITE

Several of CNN's employees who were pilots became good friends. One of these was John Holliman, a member of the original reporting corps for CNN. He rose to prominence as one of CNN's "Boys of Baghdad" during the first Persian Gulf War in 1991, and was one of only three journalists reporting from Baghdad when Allied bombing of the city began. He was later known for his coverage of science, technology, and space exploration.

Another CNN pilot friend was Miles O' Brien. He is a third-generation private pilot. His father, also a private pilot, shared his love of flying with Miles at an early age. Miles's first flights were in Cessnas and Pipers that his father rented. Additionally, Miles's paternal and maternal grandfathers were also private pilots. While with CNN in Atlanta and New York, Miles served as CNN's science, space, aviation technology, and environment correspondent. He anchored programs including Science and Technology Week, Headline News, Primetime, CNN Live, and CNN American Morning.

Another friend at CNN was Tom Gaut. Tom was a prominent director at CNN, having come on board when CNN first went on the air. He directed several presidential debates, including feeds to the national press pool. We were frequently honored to be guests of Tom's in the control room during these debates. Eventually, Tom came to work at King Schools as a director.

We have frequently been interviewed on air by CNN as subject matter experts when aviation events occurred.

When John Glenn was scheduled to return to space, CNN selected

John Holliman to anchor the event. Then CNN and Holliman invited Walter Cronkite to co-anchor the event. Walter said he would do it because of his friendship with John Holliman, but he was to receive an award from the United Nations the evening before and it would not be practical for him to fly down to Florida on the airlines. CNN asked if John and I would be willing to fly Walter and his chief of staff, Marlene Adler, to Florida the evening before the event, which we agreed to do.

Sadly, a few weeks before the event, John Holliman was going out to buy waffle syrup for breakfast and was killed in a head-on collision. CNN asked Walter if they could substitute Miles O' Brien for John Holliman. Walter was distressed and said that his deal was with John, not Miles, and he didn't know Miles. Miles flew to meet Walter and was able to restore the commitment. Miles came back as the conquering hero with the deal back on again. We did fly Walter to Merritt Island, Florida. On the flight, I was the captain and John was my co-pilot. As the airplane climbed after takeoff, the en-route charts that were between us slid to the back of the airplane and landed between Walter's feet. John was assigned the job of retrieving them. As John knelt to recover them, Walter said, "Oh, just fly south." If only it were that easy!

During the event, Walter and Miles were on a riser with cameras aimed at them. We were fortunate to be on either side of them, just out of camera sight. As you may know, the crew speaks to on-camera talent through earpieces referred to as interruptible feed-backs (IFB). Walter complained that the IFB was not loud enough for him to hear. It must have been reasonably loud—John and I could both hear it.

This inability to hear proved to be a great challenge to Walter in covering the event. It greatly limited his ability to dialogue with the astronauts. If the astronauts were to ask Walter a question he would not be able to hear it, so all the questions were pre-scripted and no follow-up questions were allowed. Walter found this very frustrating. When CNN asked him if he would be willing to do it again, Walter said, "No, never."

Martha

Walter Cronkite had a warm sense of humor.

ACKNOWLEDGMENTS

One of the greatest pleasures in life is to associate with competent, ethical people. Larry Becker fills the bill. It has been our habit when we do something that is new to us, that we hire someone who knows more about the subject than we do.

Larry is a great case in point. We had written/produced exactly zero books. Larry had done at least three. He had knowledge we desperately needed. He managed the editing and production of this book with grace and unpretentiousness, and in the process became our trusted friend.

Larry, thanks so much for all you have done for us. You are great to collaborate with, good friend.